Contents
i

Editorial
iii

Editorial

Welcome to our tenth issue! Five years is a long time in new writing, and a milestone in the life of a small literary journal. When we launched back in 2009, it was our gentle aim to "take a risk now and then" in a creative scene that had become, well, a little boring, trivial, insular and bland. We changed things by being serious, exciting and diverse. Much of the credit for this goes to those 337 writers who have appeared in our 1612 pages since then, but we are honoured to have provided a nexus, a supportive white space for the written arts. There are many individuals we want to thank, most of whom know who they are, but in particular, for their advice and support at various points in our history, Patricia Ace, Sally Evans Kirsty Gunn, Alexander Hutchison, Ian Jack, Tom Leonard, Bob McDevitt, Maggie McKernan, Helena Nelson, Lauren Nicoll, Michael Schmidt, Alan Warner and the late Gavin Wallace – not forgetting our partners and families for tolerating the biannual flooding of our homes and lives with a tide of white A4.

Those unfamiliar with our February 2009 launch editorial perhaps too narrowly interpret this magazine's title in the reductive meaning of a 'gutter press'. Yes we wanted our readers to sniff Scotland's literary effluence, but also to publish visceral prose, and support poetry lit by the liminal glow of a *gutter*ing candle. Most importantly, we wanted to grow a readership that smelt the fine ink in the *gutter* of our inner margins and realise that there was still a future on paper. And grow we have, from our initial circulation of 400 to a steady readership and contributorship from across the Scottish diasporas.

As you might know, 2/3 of *Gutter*'s editorial staff has a scientific background. We like data, so we ran the numbers: in ten issues, we have published 228 pieces of new prose and 474 new poems. To distil that down from the raw submissions pile, we estimate we read over 2 million words of new prose and several thousand lines of poetry.

We published 169 men, 166 women and two people whose gender we could not distinguish from their biography... Almost three-quarters of our contributors are based in Scotland, followed by Switzerland (is it the Toblerone?), Spain, the US, England, Canada, and Japan. Although we are a new writing journal, most writers who are published in *Gutter* already have track record: a whopping 89.9% had been previously published in another journal, and 41% had released at least one book. And we don't just publish the same writers over and over: each issue had an average of 37 writers making their debut in the magazine.

All very interesting, but in our commitment to new writing, are we encouraging the right people? Well, between them, our 337 contributors have published 47 new books since their *Gutter* debut. From *Gutter* has grown Freight Books, which this year launches an ambitious list of 27 new titles, and this magazine shared its founding Zeitgeist with the rise of other new Scottish publishers such as Saraband, Sandstone and Cargo Publishing, many of whose authors have found voice in these pages. Finally, 7 of our contributors have won subsequently major prizes or awards for their work – this is probably an underestimate as we have been relying on the brag-o-sphere for information, but in the near future we will be emailing out an alumni survey to see if we are meeting our aspiration to be a forum where writers can "experiment, develop and flourish".

What would we do differently if we had our time again? Probably we would have tried harder to find a wealthy sponsor to help us commission new work and foster a culture of professionalism where writers can expect a reasonable fee for their labours. Alas, financial insecurity remains part of the romance of running a journal, but we would like to extend our deepest gratitude to our regular subscribers, our advertisers, and our principal funders Creative Scotland and Glasgow Arts for their faith in our vision for Scottish publishing.

It is also a constant source of regret that time constraints prevent us from entering into a more regular dialogue with our contributors. All the editorial staff are unpaid, lack a large inheritance and are thus compelled to maintain day jobs. We like to think we have a good gauge of the work we are sent, but who knows what startling discoveries we might have brought you if we'd only had more time to engage with work that 'just wasn't quite ready' for publication. Dialogue is of course vital when it comes to setting the agenda in any artistic endeavour. It is through such discourse that avants-gardes develop, and that is something we will be mindful of over our next ten issues.

Which brings us neatly to the relaunch. No doubt you have already noticed that the magazine that you hold in you hands bears little resemblance to the three-colour typography and columnar layout of its predecessors. While the award-winning original design caught eyes and pleased bookshelves, it was time for a change.

In the spirit of discourse mentioned above, we have also introduced a regular author interview, where writers can hold forth on their art. And for your delectation, we include a new agony column for all your inky wee secrets.

Regular readers will notice a lot of new names in this issue. In particular, we draw your attention to short stories from Kate Tregaskis and Nick Athanasiou. We are also glad to have new work from Zoë Wicomb, Ruth Thomas, Kevin MacNeil and Zoë Strachan. Women dominate the magazine as never before, reflecting the great strength of talent available.

In poetry, Alan Spence shows us the Moon in three poems while David Crystal takes us to North Africa and back via the local kebab shop. We are delighted to have Tim Turnbull making his first appearance in these pages, and Brian Johnstone joins the circus with a selection of poems from his 'Ring Cycle'. There is also a great selection of new pieces by regulars Kate Tough, Lindsay Macgregor, Olive M Ritch, Judith Taylor and Jim Carruth.

Gutter is cosmopolitan in spirit and our editorial staff spend a lot of time wandering the continent by bus and budget airline, either seeking inspiration or growing sales. Recently in Berlin, we were struck by multi-page features in that city's two best selling arts magazines which were devoted to the phenomenon of new vibrant publishing houses. Imagine both *The List* and *The Skinny* promoting new Scottish publishing across several pages? And yet we convince ourselves that the scene here is just as vibrant, only a little shorter on cash. The true nature of the difference? We have lost our 'reading culture', the mulch in which new ideas (for what else is a book?) can take root and find an independent audience. It began with the demise of the net-book agreement, and it continues with the loss of bookshops as places of communication – however excellent they may be, book festivals are too thinly spread a substrate. In Germany and much of continental Europe, there still exist distinct cultures of creation and reception that thrive around the local independent bookshop. But in Scotland, emerging literary culture is becoming circular, autophagic and almost expects no paying audience, for that is what it has now been conditioned to expect. Outwith that culture remain the old cadres of the high literati and a disengaged public who suspect the serious young literary artist may be some sort of confidence trickster. Perhaps that was always the case, but it is magnified by the loss of any expectation of a fair transaction. A tall order then: as well as promoting new work, to recreate the environment for serious reading.

While culture is a living, mutable thing, individuals are perhaps too inclined to follow the easy path. *Gutter* was recently at a country funeral, and hearing the older folk converse in Scots brought us in mind of the last lines of Louis Zukovsky's poem 'Autobiography', and the poet's lifelong unease at his growing alienation from his Yiddish roots through assimilation into a modern, American-English, secular culture. It ends with the line "Keine Kadish [sic] wird man sagen", which is a reference to Heinrich Heine's poem 'Gedächtnisfeier' (Memorial), where Heine laments: "Keine Messe wird man singen, / Keinen Kadosch wird man sagen, / Nichts gesagt und nichts gesungen / Wird an meinen Sterbetagen". To translate: "No Mass will anyone sing / Nor Kaddish will anyone speak, / Nothing will be said and nothing sung / When come my dying days".

As with Yiddish, so with Scots? No? What of the latest results from the 2013 census that show nearly 1.5 million users of our own old Germanic tongue? But the problem there is one of definition. Such figures belie a sad ebbing away of a once vibrant verbal culture. We are losing our idiom and before long will have only the redundant adjectives – who of us with just our smattering of "wees" and "happits" will sing, let alone compose a lament? It is therefore with delight that this issue includes two rich pieces of Scots prose, with idiomatic translations into English available on the *Gutter* website for your education. We are less than a generation from a situation of near-total language loss. Learn it or lose it!

Stamped below the image were the offensive words in handwriting font: Glamour Puss. When she was promoted to Matron, a group of nurses presented her with the mug. Letty smiled warmly, even as her blood turned to ice.

Art Work
Zoë Wicomb

Art Work

Zoë Wicomb

If that blinking boy doesn't get out of bed today, Letty muttered to herself, then... She looked about the kitchen, bewildered. For a moment the room had morphed into Brenda's kitchen in Manenberg, Brenda bustling about to conceal the lump in her throat, and she, Letty, running her hand over the cracked red formica of the table. She stood up, firmly pushed back her chair to dispel the image. Well, she'd give him until ten o'clock, couldn't say fairer than that. Gripping her mug of coffee, Letty thought determination. Leo was her responsibility, so a solution simply had to be found. Of course, it wasn't easy, she'd be the first to acknowledge that, not easy at all growing up in this place where all expectations have gone to pot. No jobs to be found, but no point in being picky, you've got to buckle down to work of any kind, even if you think it beneath you. Art, after all, was working with the hands. Letty knew plenty of people who needed odd jobs done, painting and decorating, a bit of carpentry, and so on. Otherwise, what lay ahead was a life of lying on your back, building castles in the air. That, unfortunately, was the kind of thing artists easily fell into, so if that boy was not out of bed by ten, she would have to...

Resolve – that was the thing to see them through, that in the past had seen her through, propelled her into a tolerable life. The thing was... Or rather, the correct thing to do...

Leo was hers, had been since the age of eleven when Brenda sent him to her in Glasgow where he would escape the gangsters of Manenberg and the sure influence of tik. It may have been the New South Africa with its rainbow nation but, as far as her sister Brenda could see, the end of that rainbow promised nothing other than a crock of kak. Leo, blade sharp as he was, would simply not survive in that hell's furnace where children stumbled about the township streets, drugged on tik.

Letty had missed the boat. That was the irksome expression that Brenda used, as if there were something wonderful about being married to a light-skinned layabout with pressed hair. Fat Brenda in a housecoat with too many children, broken backed with the bailing out of water, but supremely satisfied on her second leaky boat. Letty knew not to protest; she was no longer young, and marriage and children were after all unlikely, especially in the cold dark country where she had made her home. Brenda said that life without a child was not healthy. Bullshit, Letty thought, but given that Brenda could spare Leo, an odd, contrary child who did not get on with his stepfather, she bit her lip and rose to the challenge. Now, after all these years, Leo was hers.

As a nurse, Letty could afford to live only in the East End of the city where the schools, she believed, were not up to much, but how fortunate that in those days she could rely on the local children to shun an African boy. Leo was tall and strong so she reckoned they would leave him alone, keep their drugs and bevvy to themselves, whilst she would keep him on the straight and narrow. And look how well he's done minding his own business, flying through school, even if art school had been a great disappointment to Letty who had hoped that the boy with his excellent grades would look to medicine. A fine mouthful that would have been: my son, Leo, the doctor.

Art! She could not stop herself from declaiming the word over and over. Art was a healthy hobby, something good to do in your spare time, but what about a job, a proper profession? Where will art take you? she asked. It was infuriating, after all that schooling, even if there was little left these days of what was once known as the best of British. But the boy shrugged, and in that toneless voice of the young said that he had not in mind any special place to go. It was just as well to remember that theirs was the best art school in the country, he said formally.

Letty noted with pleasure his identification with the school and the city – even his accent was by now overlaid with Scottish. No, Brenda no longer had any claim on him. And it was the case that the graduation ceremony at the grand old university, followed by strawberries on the lawn, was a magnificent event that she would not have missed for all the world, with Leo for once attentive by her side, because if the truth be told it was uncomfortable being stared at by old white men. Never mind if they whimpered to her for bedpans or to have their bottoms wiped; here they stared rudely. Leo shushed her. Gotta chill, he said. They were hardly the same geezers whose bums she had come across at the Infirmary.

Letty had once seen a crazy looking, drunken woman make a fool of herself on television. There was no telling what the person wanted to say, youngish she was too, but oh, speaking was her thing, even as she slurred and gesticulated and interrupted others on the panel. And in a common English voice too. She turned out to be an artist. Heavens, if that was what Leo had in mind he might as well have stayed in Manenberg. And Letty had been right about art school. Nowadays, having graduated, Leo had nothing better to do than hang about with that Ashraf boy, talking nonsense about the coordinates of space and time – language chosen, she suspected, to annoy her. Soon, they would get a space together, they wittered, as if they did not have perfectly good homes. Talking and waiting, that was their thing, except for the night jobs in bars. And while Leo waited, he thought it acceptable to spend days in bed, or at least in his room, dallying with depression, she imagined, or other such namby-pamby European nonsense.

I'm reading, he would say, or even more infuriatingly, Go away, I'm thinking, and she had a horrible suspicion that he and Ashraf were up to no good. When Ashraf arrived a few weeks ago with a beard, her heart sank. If that boy is training to be a terrorist, she screamed at Leo, I'd be marching the both of you straight to the police station. Yo, Leo sighed, chill man, it's only a dare. Ash is too much of a Becks man to fall for fundamentalism. But Letty barely slept until the boy shaved his disgusting beard. Becks boy he might be, but she was alert to the dangers of this world. No, a solution had to be found for Leo – and her eyes roved helplessly about the crowded kitchen shelves – even if it took a second mug of coffee, an indulgence she rarely allowed herself.

Letty's mug is adorned with a drawing of a fancy woman with pouting red lips and yellow hair with flick-ups – like the photo-romans she used to read voraciously at school. Penny Horribles the malicious teachers called them, confiscating the booklets that the girls passed on to each other, feverish for romance. Leo called the mug her Lichtenstein. Stamped below the image were the offensive words in handwriting font: Glamour Puss. When she was promoted to Matron, a group of nurses presented her with the mug. Letty smiled warmly, even as her blood turned to ice. She said it was lovely, promised that from that day on her morning coffee at home would be drunk out of nothing else. She rose majestically and slowly, deliberately rolling her hips grown wide with age, made her way to the locker where once again she held up the mug admiringly before slipping it into her bag. Thank you, she said graciously, it will have pride of place in my home.

There was a lesson in it, she pronounced to Leo. If people try to make fun of you, embrace the insult, nuzzle and squeeze the sting out of it, make it your own, she explained. No fucking chance (God forgive her language) of a daily giggle to be had at her expense, at her raised mug there at the nurses' station. Letty could play the game as coolly as any – a flat bottom and a white face were not required for strategic thinking, she explained to Leo, who rolled his eyes. More importantly she would not shirk from keeping her word, she persisted. From that day her morning coffee was indeed drunk from the Glamour Puss mug which, having lost its odium, its sting, became a favourite.

Leo was not as loyal or sympathetic as he ought to have been. Yo, he said, I can just imagine how those people are driven crazy with all your preaching about compassion and cleanliness and work, work, work. I reckon you came off lightly with that mug. And off he went, slamming the door. But that evening he arrived with a box of Black Magic chocolates, made Ovaltine in the Glamour Puss mug, and put on her favourite CD. She's a Black Magic Woman, Leo crooned along as he whirled her around the room, instead of raising his eyebrows at what he called her weird music, and a lovely evening it was too, even if he did drink a beer straight out of the bottle, which she thought uncivilised, and for all her prodding managed to say nothing at all about himself.

Letty turned her second mug of coffee this way and that; she could swear that the glamour puss winked and mouthed an answer. Yes, that was it, she knew just how to lick him into shape. Unless Leo found a job by the end of that very week, any job, he would have to pack up and leave. Which, of course, he couldn't do. Where would he go? She had raised him to have pride, never to stoop to social benefits or charity, so she could rely on him not to sneak his way into social housing. Get up or else, she'd threaten, in the knowledge that he would not want to go back to Cape Town. The visits home, she knew, had become increasingly difficult, nothing more than a chore for him. Letty did not relish the thought of bullying, but what to do, what to do in the face of such moral danger?

She had given in on church when Leo explained that his god of righteousness came with a small g and did not require worshipping. A load of uppity bullshit, encouraged by art school, oh she knew that all right, but the maxim of embracing that which offends came to her rescue. What chance had she against modern godlessness? Strategist as she prided herself to be, she bit the bullet, had to chill, as Leo said, for the choice between God and her boy could only lead to eternal damnation. At least Leo was not on drugs, did not even smoke cigarettes, and had not succumbed to Glasgow drinking.

Having drained the mug and tapped the temple of the glamour puss, Letty rose, knocked at Leo's door, prepared to barge in and wake him up. Hey, he called. The boy, dressed and sitting at his desk hunched over a sketchbook, did not look up. I wondered if you wanted coffee, she improvised. There's warm porridge on the stove. Nah, he said abstractedly. Er, no thanks. Christ, sorry, I had no idea of the time. Must fly.

Letty should have rejoiced, but really, she couldn't help feeling that there was something fishy about the job Leo claimed to be rushing off to. Didn't I tell you about the interview? he said, disingenuously, brushing past her. Och, it's nothing much, just some work for this Swiss artist, a temporary job for the month of the Edinburgh Festival, and off he rushed, slamming the door.

Young men are difficult, touchy, and there's no calculating the degree of delicacy needed to deal with them, Rosalie, her Jamaican friend at church, declared. Rosalie was full of airs and graces and fancy talk. She had both son and daughter; she assured Letty that for all the talk about female capriciousness, her Saul was by far the more fickle, more difficult. There was no accounting for his belief that the world was his oyster, for the impatience, the moods, or the temper that flared as soon as something did not go his way. Letty was best advised to let Leo be, not to ask too many questions. Letty looked at her askance. As if Leo were anything like that pretentious boy of Rosalie's. Still, she couldn't help thinking that there was furtiveness about his movements, an unusual guardedness about his replies.

So what did he actually do at the festival? All sorts, Leo said briskly, evasively. There's a whole lot of construction, yeh, and maintenance work. Since when are you interested in art? he asked, fobbing her off. It would have been nice to know at least whether this temporary work was likely to lead somewhere, but perhaps Rosalie was right, so Letty did not persist; she would try another time. But the boy was hardly ever home these days. Even Ashraf called round wondering where he was, why he had not returned his calls.

Last night, Leo, normally tidy, even fastidious, had left his parka flung down on the sofa. Letty hauled it to the cupboard and heard the thud of a booklet falling out of the pocket. It was a Festival brochure folded at the Exhibitions section, and she could see no harm in having a look. There was the listing of exhibitions, and she recognised, since it was also an Afrikaans name, that of Leo's Swiss artist. It was some kind of performance as far as she could tell, although the description might as well have been in Greek, for she could make neither head nor tail of it. Like that woman on television who couldn't talk sense – in which case she supposed that the woman might not have been drunk after all. That seemed to be the way with art: couldn't be explained in plain English, and nothing at all to do with beauty, as she discovered at Leo's degree show, no nice pictures on the wall of things you could recognise. Yo, Leo had agreed unhelpfully, no fleece-covered hot water bottles to be found here.

Sitting at the kitchen table that morning, bathed in buttery yellow light, Letty felt the warmth, the grace of summer sunlight demanding something special of her. She had not been to Edinburgh for years, let alone the Festival, but on this lovely day, why not? Why not ring to see if Rosalie would come along? But Rosalie complained that she had ironing to do, no time for looking at pictures, that modern art was not her thing. It's not modern art, Letty explained haughtily, echoing Leo; it's called contemporary art, and has nothing at all to do with pictures. Rosalie said, well then, there you are, emperor's clothes was her understanding, so please could she be excused.

If only Rosalie were not so spiritless, for it took some determination for Letty to hop all by herself on to the bus, and then the train from Queen Street. How surprised Leo would be, at her who never went anywhere – and pleased too, she hoped. She would go the exhibition at Summerhall, then, according to the brochure, there was plenty jollity to be had on the streets with jugglers and musicians and whatnot; no need even to spend a cent more than her train fare. Well, she might stretch to a cup of tea and a nice cream bun. Or perhaps just a bar of chocolate and a cool drink on a bench in the sun, no point in being indoors when it's bright and balmy, and she held up her hands, turned her wrists in anticipation of delicious sunlight. Lovely enough it was to kick off one's shoes in the sun.

Having arrived at the exhibition hall, Lettie is no longer sure about the navy Per Una suit and church shoes with a little heel. Perhaps not the most sensible footwear for exploring a festival, but she had in mind not to embarrass Leo with sloppy dress. Here she is surrounded by people who have deliberately dressed down. There are even a few outlandish youths with piercings and tattoos that make her wince for the pain, and the only late middle-aged couple in the group – surely in their gardening clothes – studiously avoid looking at her. Which, she must say, is more civilised than staring. Rather than being huddled together in this grubby anteroom, Letty expected to be shown into a pristine white space with people milling about, peering at improbable structures. Where she would not be conspicuous, although she has to smile at that. Looking as she does, her head gridded into interlocking plaits with coloured beads randomly woven in – cost a pretty packet too – she supposes she cannot escape notice.

A sharp young woman in a security guard's uniform shouts into a walkie-talkie, claps her hands briskly, and shepherds the motley group into a queue. Only one person will be let in at a time, she bellows, and you have only five minutes in the exhibition. Once you enter, keep going and feel free to open all the doors you find. When you leave the space at the other end, and she taps her walkie-talkie, the next person will enter.

Letty believes that for all the nonsense people talk, especially the over-educated ones, there is lucid language in everyone's eyes, if only you took the trouble to look and read carefully. But she is baffled by the guard or guide who, for all her candid look, has drawn a veil across her eyes. Something to hide – what other explanation could there be? Something odd at play, Letty fears, so that the warmth of the day turns on her and a horrible heat rises from her feet to her collar. If only she could kick off her shoes, but the guard shakes her head with clairvoyant precision, and Letty blushes. There is no going back without making a fool of herself, besides, the brisk guard will not have her line disrupted.

The time goes all too quickly; the walkie-talkie crackles, announcing a departure at the other end, and now dear God it is her turn. Letty's soles have melded into the vinyl floor. She cannot move, but the devious, dumb-eyed guard, switching on a mechanical smile, says, Come along now, and taking a deep breath Letty finds her shoes released, her feet propelled forward.

In the corridor – not the cleanest she has come across – she is pleased to be on her own. On the right is a door that she ought to open. Gingerly, she turns the handle, but no, it is locked, and Letty cannot help feeling relief. Although, if the whole thing turns out to be a joke of closed doors, an exercise in prohibition, as if she has not had enough of that in the bad old days in Cape Town, she would not be best pleased, and what's more, where is Leo in all this? She ought to have asked the guard about Leo, that may well have taken her by surprise, made language leap unbidden into her eyes.

Here, on the left is another door to try. This time it opens, and as it shuts behind her Letty falls back against it, blinded by whiteness. It is hardly a room determined by walls; no, this is pure space, an empty, uniform whiteness spread all around, with cold, dazzling light that seems to come from nowhere, stripping every inch of the space of – oh, she does not know of what. She steps forward into the nothingness, to what may well be the centre, and is engulfed by something indefinable, something like terror. Or is it grief? Instinctively, her body reverses in slow motion towards the door, expecting to be prevented, to be kept captive in the empty whiteness. Her hand gropes behind her back for the door handle, and she stumbles out, gasping for air. Was there a white gas of some kind swirling around? Strangely, the sensation of suffocating gas comes retrospectively, and she can't be sure.

Ahead, at the end of the corridor, there is another white door, grubby around the handle, and if she is not mistaken there are people talking on the other side. Which is anything but reassuring. Letty wonders if it is a recording, but as she approaches, the noise amplifies, sounds more real. Certainly people talking, laughing, and she feels anxious about entering a roomful of jovial strangers. Then, as her hand turns the door handle, the sound stops abruptly.

It is as if a wind propels her into the room, black as the blackest night. The walls must be painted black, leeching light out of the space, and Letty, disorientated, blinded and blinking to adjust, prefers to think of retinal rods and cones clacking as they change guard. But they rise out of the darkness all the same, the figures that take human form: the bodies of young black men, naked, entirely still as if frozen in midspeech. So, they have stopped talking, stopped joking amongst themselves to see her, Laetitia Wilson, frozen in horror. God in heaven, what has she done to deserve this... this abomination; it is she who is on display; it is she who might as well be standing there naked with the new rolls of flesh around her stomach, her swollen hips and dimpled bottom, wobbling in shame. Letty drops her eyes, but even on the floor lies a naked black body looking not exactly at her, but looking all the same, expressionless like the rest of them, so that she looks up once more, careful not to rest her eyes on any private parts. The black room bristles with private parts made public. Boiling with outrage, she has to get out, quickly, but then recovers. Not before giving these boys a bit of her mind. Get your clothes on, at once. Have you no shame? Get your disgusting selves home right away. This is what she shouts, what they ought to hear, but no words agree to leave her lips.

Like an automaton, a mute Letty steers herself through the bodies to the door – she has to get out. As her hand falls on the handle, her eyes fall on Leo standing impassively to the right. Her eyes bore into the side of his head; her voice fails even as her lips move. Leo stares fixedly ahead. If she can't speak, she will wallop him with her handbag, but as she raises her arm to strike, a male guard in uniform takes her elbow. Next one please, he says into his walkie-talkie, and the door shuts behind her.

Letty grabs his sleeve. Her voice returns. No, no, no, she shouts, she needs to get back in there, needs to speak to those disgraceful boys, find them some clothes, switch on the lights. Do they think they can't be seen in the dark? She will not have it, will not be shamed in this way in the city of Edinburgh.

No chance, says the guard, who now has a firm grip on her arm. Letty shouts over his Shush madam, shush. Where are those UKBA thugs now? she screams. Always picking up the wrong people, decent people, instead of taking these shameful boys away. Fly them back home, to the homes of their grandparents, out of this... this Sodom and Gomorrah of shameful art. The guard steers her towards the stairs. Letty, drained, cannot resist. She too wants to be flown back home. How could she ever hold up her head again? How could Leo do such a thing – what for? Stripping like a prostitute for money? He'd be better off in Manenberg, reeling on tik, rather than taking his clothes off for white folks.

The guard says, Pull yourself together, Missus. It's only art, only a wee bunch of guys with their dicks out. There's a café up there. Get a wee cuppa and calm down, and he darts back to take his place at the door.

A wee cuppa? A cup of tea? Imagine sitting down to tea whilst Babel comes crashing down! Blindly, through blinding heat, she finds her way back to Waverley station. At home she kicks off her Sunday shoes and waits in the sitting room with arms folded, stiffly in her navy suit. She does not draw the curtains, does not turn on the light when the gloam sets in; she has neither hunger nor thirst. There is too much to think through, too much bewilderment to register the cooling of the night. Like heroines from bygone days she sits in her loneness, contemplates the hard floor, the cold grate, and thinks of betrayal in its myriad forms. She will not light a candle for her midnight meditation. She will come through.

Leo comes home in the pearly light of dawn, fully clothed. Sit, she orders calmly. Rosalie warned me of the emperor's clothes, she says. Is that what you're acting out? No, let me start with the interview. Given that you do nothing but stand about in your birthday suits, was the interview about measuring you boys? Tell me, did you have yourself measured like a Castle Hottentot?

Leo splutters, tries not to laugh. Yo, you've got to chill, he says. Of course we weren't measured. Wrong end of the stick, but you're getting there. Stand the emperor on his head, get him somersaulting a couple of times, and we'll get there. Look, he says, pulling a box out of his bag, chocolates for a black magic woman.

Gregor Schneider's *Süßer Duft* (Sweet Scent) was exhibited at the Edinburgh Festival 2013

There are some things still beautiful in Africa

Lynnda Wardle

The brown envelopes arrive every three months or so, addressed to him in his father's hand which is still neat although a little shaky. They are stuffed with news clippings detailing the events of everyday life in his home town of Johannesburg; murders, muggings, rapes; crimes that have money as their motive, but have a random brutality that he finds shocking. He cannot bear to read them, or his father's careful pencil annotations: Lucas, you have no idea! See what we have to put up with? Or, a picture of a busy shopping mall, the escalators cordoned off with police tape: Only last week at the Cresta Shopping Centre! Your mother and I saw the bullet holes. Nothing has been fixed. And the unwritten line: It could have been us.

Although he acknowledges the truth of these reports, it is a world far away from his own. In his world, he sometimes forgets to lock his front door as he leaves the flat and comes back to find it undisturbed, everything neatly in its place. The entrance still smells of last night's dinner, the clock ticks softly on the kitchen wall. His neighbours in the close scold him about his forgetfulness and tell him stories of Glasgow to caution him. It is as though he is trying safety out for size. He feels safe here and safety has become his expectation. He is no longer startled if a jogger surprises him from behind, he carries his wallet tucked in his back pocket and has stopped hiding money in his sock when he goes out.

He leaves the latest envelope unopened for a week. Finally on the Saturday after it arrives, he lifts it off the hall mat where it has become scuffed and damp and heads to the kitchen for a cup of coffee, regretting that he has to spend an hour of his day off in this way. The sky appears dark even though it is nearly ten in the morning and the hawthorn tree outside his window looks sodden after a night of rain. He flicks through the clippings quickly: Old woman mugged on the way to have hair done in Northcliff. Elderly couple shot dead in driveway. Woman disturbs burglars. Three month old baby shot and left for dead. This time, his father has included a picture of a baobab tree, solid against the blue sky and a neat pencilled arrow with the spidery text: Lucas – included this because there are some things still beautiful in Africa! He feels thirsty and stands at the sink letting the tap run, dangling his fingers under the cold water. He imagines that one day there will not be an envelope, but a phone call to pull him back to Johannesburg and the heart of their misery.

Mr Burger?

The voice will have the tell-tale flattening of the vowels; the 'r' in Burger rolled quickly and expertly – an Afrikaner's pronunciation. It will have been a tragedy: two men with their caps pulled down and collars turned up will have darted into the property as his father struggles with the padlock on the gate. They will grab the old man from behind, tie him up and steal his keys, pull his mother from the car, run from room to room, stuffing clothes, food and jewellery into big canvas bags.

We're sorry, Mr Burger, your parents have been killed.

It is this word that holds fear for him – a cruel jagged word that makes him feel breathless when he hears it even casually on the news. He is about five, living with his parents in a sagging Art Deco residential hotel in Pretoria with portholes for windows and curving white staircases. The Hotel Vincent – a grand colonial name for what was really a glorified boarding house where they stay when his father starts a new job. The gardens are overshadowed by jacaranda trees in the summer, and small tubs of orange nasturtiums and purple vygies mark the entrance. The crescent shape, he thinks now, is reminiscent of the old Boer laager, protecting the weak on the inside, designed to keep the enemy at bay. His father works in the advertising section of a large department store and he overhears his parents talking about promotion and getting a bond for a new house, but they have been here two years and they live with the possibility of being sent back to Johannesburg at any time.

Lucas doesn't want to go back. He is an only child and suddenly finds himself the youngest in a group of fourteen or more children. He discovers the joys of being a pack animal roaming the grounds, playing tok-tokkie on the doors of elderly residents, involved in games of hide and seek where sometimes he is forgotten by the others. He hears their voices disappearing as they go back to their flats while he continues to crouch under a cool hydrangea bush his insides rumbling with excitement, waiting to be discovered. The families all eat together in a communal dining hall, things that he now supposes one might find on a boarding school menu: tomato bredie and rice with cucumber salad, jam roly-poly pudding with custard. The dining hall has a sweet bready smell that permeates his clothes.

Their flat looks out onto clipped gardens to the front. If he stands on the wooden chair in the kitchen he can see out to the back alley where the hotel staff have their quarters. The boys' rooms. Lying in his bed at night he occasionally hears talking and laughter floating up the alley and smells paraffin and cooking meat. Now and again he catches scraps of words he understands from Zulu or Sotho: wena, tjaaila or sometimes, jislaaik or fok, the forbidden Afrikaans words that his father will use when he is angry. His mother wants to move to another flat where they will not have to listen to the blacks' geraas, their noise, every night. His father only shrugs and says that they will soon be moving one way or the other.

This Saturday has been cold and the lawns are dry and brown. His lips are cracked from the wind and he is glad to have come in from playing outside to sit by the small two-bar heater and listen to the radio. He is careful not to burn the pom-poms on the tops of his slippers. His grandmother has sent him a hand knitted sweater from Cape Town that is rough and uncomfortable. She knits one every year, but this year she has miscalculated how much he has grown and the sleeves are too short. He starts to scratch. His mother puts down her whisky sour.

That's them starting up again Etienne, she says.

It's pay day. His father shakes his head. Bloody kaffirs. Drink and fight as soon as they get some money in their pockets.

Lucas stares out at the scrappy pink and orange sunset staining the sky. He feels frightened by the noises from the alley and the tone of his father's voice. His father stands up quickly, pulling on a sweater.

I'm going to tell them to pipe down. This is a decent hotel. We don't have to put up with this kind of thing.

Etienne for godssakes, she says. Leave them alone. We don't want any trouble.

His father leaves and clatters down the stairs. Lucas runs to the kitchen window and pulls up the wooden chair. He sees his father's bald head bobbing towards the servants' quarters. A door opens and a slice of yellow light flares in the alley. The noise of voices is suddenly louder and then quiet again as his father is swallowed inside the room. Everything is silent. He runs to the lounge, and now to his shame, tears stream down his face.

He will be killed! He is shouting at his mother. Do something, they will kill him!

She hits him hard across his mouth, her face inches from his own and he can smell the sweetness on her breath.

Don't ever use that word, Lucas, do you hear me? she hisses. Ever.

In the dining room the next day the waiters are deferential and tease him a little as usual.

Another pudding Kleinbaas Lucas! You are such a big boy!

They are neatly dressed in the white waiting uniform, their starched dish cloths draped over their arms. Lucas notices the dressings covering an eye, a cheek, a bandaged arm. His parents say nothing and he is left imagining the sudden pink of their torn skin, the darkness of their blood against the white uniform. He remembers thinking then that black people must have different blood to his own. He cannot understand that these men were wounded and somehow his father had returned unharmed.

Lucas thinks now of the sprawling house in which his parents still live alone, barricaded by high white walls. His parents are stubborn and will not move. They speak as though these incidents could only happen to other people, outside the safety of their fortress, and as though this could not happen to them. Lucas remembers that in the last letter his father had mentioned the installation of a new electronic system that involved a complicated set of entry codes. The alarm protection was to be backed up by rough men from the armed response company they paid each month to guard the property. He had forgotten this detail. He revisits the scenario. The burglars would have to detain his parents at the gate and demand entry. He closes his eyes. He can see his father reaching for the small handgun under the driver's seat and his mother trembling, trying to work the remote for the new electronic gate. It would be futile.

Lucas shifts the news cuttings around and picks up the picture of the baobab tree. The upside down tree. Its branches finger a cloudless sky, its trunk rooted in hard soil. The replies he has been drafting in his head to his father have lost their shape. He thinks about calling instead. It is still early, but he feels tired and at a loss as to what to do with his day. Perhaps he will call later. He stuffs the clippings back into the envelope and leaves the flat, pulling his hood up against the rain.

Mr Lion

Kate Tregaskis

'Well hello Mr Lion,' Ronnie says from inside the zoo enclosure. The guy approaching the fence is wearing a plastic lion mask. 'Ha, ha, very funny,' Ronnie says. It'll be someone he knows, taking the piss.

The guy in the mask stops in front of the fence. 'Ronnie Watts, Homo sapien. Performance Artist,' he says, reading the sign in front of Ronnie's enclosure. 'Diet mainly fruit and vegetables. Ronnie will be resident in the zoo during December and January.'

There's a large hole in the mask for the mouth, he can see the man's lips moving. Ronnie doesn't recognise the voice, doesn't recognise what's visible of the man's eyes. It's disconcerting not being able to see who it is. The guy is wearing a khaki anorak, jeans, trainers, he's carrying an army surplus bag.

'Champagne huh?' Mr Lion picks up the bottle that Rebecca dumped by the path when she visited earlier. She'd brought Olly, their six-month-old son, but ended up stomping off in a huff. 'You know it's a strict no-no. No alcohol to be consumed on the premises by the beasts,' Mr Lion says, looking at the label. Like a wine waiter he shows it to Ronnie. 'Nice stuff.'

'Ha ha. My girlfriend left it. I'm trying to work out how to get it this side of the fence. I don't suppose you have any wire cutters?'

Ronnie's joking of course. At least this is alleviating the boredom. He's just realised how profoundly bored he is.

'As it happens…' Mr Lion says, pulling an impressive pair of wire cutters from his bag.

Ronnie is taken aback. His wish is this guy's command. What else is in the bag?

'What about fags? Do you have a fag on you?'

'Yeah.'

Mr Lion puts the cutters down on the path, takes a packet of Marlboro out of his bag and inserts one, together with the lighter, through the mesh.

Ronnie inhales deeply, handing back the lighter. 'Cheers. Not had one in weeks. I just really felt like one now.'

'So what's this in aid of?' Mr Lion says. 'What you doing stuck in there?'

'What do *you* think it's about?' Ronnie says. He takes a long draw on the fag, feels dizzy with pleasure, weightless. He wants another fag, wants another now, even before he's finished this one. He's opened a wound. The future is tainted by craving. Maybe Mr Lion could be persuaded to part with the packet. He wishes he'd brought money in with him for emergencies like this. The whole experience he's set up for himself is suddenly getting him down. His simple enjoyment of things – savouring the taste of raw cabbage, carrot, banana, as if for the first time, getting up with the light, going to bed when it's dark – it doesn't excite him anymore. He feels caged. Just another zoo exhibit. He wants to be with Olly. Make it up with Rebecca. Have some beers. A curry. Meat. Sit in front of the telly and let his brain melt. Doesn't want to be alone tonight on his birthday. Suddenly, badly, he wants to be free.

He pulls himself together. This feeling, it's just part of the creative process. The journey he goes on when he does a significant piece of work. And this performance *is* significant. Possibly his best work to date.

An artist friend told him, talking about the creative process, that when it gets bad, when you don't believe in it anymore, when it seems too difficult, that's when things are beginning to happen. That is when you must really push. That's when you are nearing the summit. Stagger to the top, then the exhilarating rush from the descent will come, another cycle accomplished. He just needs to push forwards, push through.

'Better stub that out,' Mr Lion says, stuffing the wire cutters back into his bag.

Coming towards them, two-by-two, is a diminutive parade of fluff, fur, felt, spines, horns, wings, claws and painted faces. The pale sunlight reveals the poor craftsmanship, stitches, Velcro, sticky tape, glue, the old pyjamas and tights. The troop of children, a woman and a priest stop in front of Ronnie's enclosure. They lower their clipboards, like alien spacecraft letting down drawbridges. Mr Lion steps to the side leaving Ronnie centre stage. There are no second glances at Mr Lion. He's normal, one of them. It's Ronnie they don't get.

'What's *he* supposed to be?'

A small boy with cardboard ears points at Ronnie.

'Is he a zookeeper?' says a small voice from behind a gorilla mask.

'Now boys and girls, this is a little detour from our Bible Trail.' The woman's voice booms from her heavily bosomed body. She nods conspiratorially at Ronnie. 'Ronnie is an artist. But instead of making paintings or sculptures, he does other things. Today he is seeing what it's like to live as one of the zoo animals.'

'Miss? What for?'

'Well, he's an artist and sometimes artists do strange things. Would anyone like to ask the artist a question?'

The woman surveys the troupe.

'Has no one got any questions for the artist?'

'Can he do any tricks?' someone asks.

'Can we go to the park?' pipes something fluffy.

'No Mary. We're here to see some of the animals God created and to fill in your worksheets. If no one has any questions, let's go and see what else we can find that's mentioned in the Bible. Wave bye-bye to the artist.'

'Bye, bye.'

The children pull up their clipboards and are led away.

Ronnie could do with another fag, he feels the loss of the last one, now an irretrievable stub the other side of the mesh. A drink too wouldn't go amiss.

Mr Lion has picked up the champagne and the cutters, offers them to him.

'Champers?'

'Wouldn't say no.' Ronnie looks around for the best place. No one need know. 'Maybe you could cut the wire here, behind this bush out of view, just enough to push the bottle through?' He could deny all knowledge.

Mr Lion is adept with the cutters; it's difficult work.

'Just big enough for the bottle. I don't want to give the impression I've tried to escape,' Ronnie laughs.

Mr Lion doesn't look up.

'Oi, it's not for me to get out, it's just to get the bottle in.'

Mr Lion grunts with the effort. The hole is getting bigger.

'Look, forget it will you. I've changed my mind. You keep the champagne.'

Mr Lion snips at the mesh.

'Listen mate, stop!' The work will be ruined in a minute. How many months down the drain? His relationship with the zoo over. Just when he's at the start of something. 'Oi!' Ronnie pushes at the other man through the mesh.

Mr Lion changes position, moves back slightly.

Ronnie's hand stings. It's bleeding. Damn. He's torn skin on the newly cut wire. The sky darkens. He looks up. A crowd has gathered. They're all wearing masks. A rhino, a chimp, a tiger, a polar bear... Not the children this time. These are grown-ups. They're dressed in black and khaki, dreadlocks, vegetarian footwear. Heads bowed they watch Mr Lion, silent except for the odd squeak and scrape of plastic. It's like a Black Mass.

Ronnie pushes at the fence again, but Mr Lion has stepped back from the range of the fence's elasticity. Ronnie looks around. Finds a stick. Tries to poke Mr Lion through the mesh.

'Want any help?'

Ronnie looks up with relief, but the guy in the rhino mask is directing his question at Mr Lion.

Mr Lion stops work. 'Nearly done. Thought we could stage the event from in here. Put the banner up against the back wall.'

There's a buzz of excitement. What is this?

'Look, who are you?'

The hole is now alarmingly big. Ronnie feels exposed.

'What are we going to do with zoo boy?' Rhino says.

Mr Lion laughs and pushes himself through the hole in the mesh into Ronnie's space. There are little puddles of stale water and sticks at their feet.

'I guess we're liberating him,' says Mr Lion looking directly at Ronnie, his eyes flickering behind the mask.

This is *Ronnie's* Everest. He was here first. He's not going to give ground just because some other guy turns up with a flag in his hand.

Ronnie throws himself at Mr Lion, tries to knee him in the groin, to snatch at his mask. But Mr Lion keeps him at arm's length, laughing. Rhino, Tiger and a chimpanzee push through the wire and are on him.

'Bastards...'

'Don't hurt him,' says Mr Lion.

Some of the masked ones push Ronnie towards the fence, others, the other side, pull him through the hole. He's been evicted from his own artwork.

'You can't do this!'

'We already have.' Rhino is laughing.

Ronnie has been dumped on the floor to one side and the rest of the masked people are squeezing through the hole in the fence into the enclosure. Ronnie kicks at the last one, eliciting a yelp. A banner is being unwound on the concrete floor of the enclosure.

Liberate!

Someone is doing handstands; others are stripping off their coats. They have t-shirts on over jumpers: Free the Animals! Stop the Cruelty! No More Zoos.

'Bastards!' Ronnie strikes the fence with his hands.

Mr Lion shakes the bottle of champagne. The cork shoots into the air. Foam spurts upwards, splatters onto the concrete.

Mr Lion lifts his mask, his face is red and sweaty, he swigs champagne, runs the back of his hand across his lips and raises the bottle, 'Cheers,' in Ronnie's direction.

Ronnie, head down, walks away. It's not fair. It was his bloody gig. He blames the zoo. What kind of protection are they providing? He could have been killed. He tries to regulate his breathing, doesn't want to be conspicuous. He can't of course come back. That's it. Finished. The performance has been ruined.

But something stirs. The tiniest flutter. Don't accept defeat. It's one of the signs of a creative mind. Be flexible. Adapt. Not problems, op-por-tun-ities.

He can turn it around. Credit for what happened is his. His eviction was the result of something he set in motion, a happening on a stage he created.

He should go back. Be on the scene. Get a disposable camera from the zoo shop. Document what's happening. This could be his best work yet.

snug

Nick Athanasiou

Finding people is easy; it's what I do. And finding Donald Cowley couldn't have been easier[1].

[NA: I hope you've read the footnote. If you haven't, I urge you to go back and do so. As eager as you might be to discover who 'I' – the narrator, not the author – is and what exactly it is that 'I do,' and who the hell Donald Cowley is and why 'I' was looking for him in the first place, I – the author, not the narrator – urge you to read the footnote. Read *all* my footnotes.]

In February, Kyle and I bought a flat in Hillhead, just behind the library. Throughout our late twenties and early thirties we'd rented a one-bed flat on the top floor of a tenement block in Partick, adhering for much of that period to the struggling-but-committed artist's dictum that all private property is theft (we would often quote Proudhon at people, the thought of which makes me cringe now). And then came success of a kind. Kyle managed to find a publisher for the novel that had taken him the best part of a decade to write, and although its publication barely caused a ripple in the literary ocean his publisher had shown enough faith in him to sign him up for two more books. For my part I was still freelancing, shooting documentaries about fat people and psychic pets that only ever aired on channels watched by people who had satellite dishes and no dignity, but I had recently embellished my CV with a three-month residency in Berlin after winning a short film prize at the Berlinale, and on the back of that I was in talks with an eminent producer about a proposal I had for a feature-length documentary[2]. This confluence of promise coincided with the death of Kyle's father, and for the first time in our lives we found ourselves blessed not only with an intoxicating optimism but – thanks to a five-figure inheritance[3] – with cash in the bank.

Practically overnight, as if we'd both awoken from the same dream, the focus of our moral indignation shifted from property-ownership *per se* to property-ownership by gluttonous, exploitative landlords; specifically, to *our* gluttonous, exploitative landlord[4]. No protracted introspection or soul-searching was needed to convince ourselves that, in our rather special

---

1   Google *Donald Cowley* in inverted commas together with *Glasgow*, and the first three results you get are '**Donald Cowley** – United Kingdom | LinkedIn', 'About Us – snug – Home Building and Renovations in Scotland' and 'snug (**Donald Cowley**) on Twitter.' Scroll down a little further and you'll find his presence on Facebook, Pinterest, MeetUp and 192.com. Click through to the second page of results and you'll find an interview with him in the Herald (probably part of a Sunday supplement) in which he's pictured leaning against his wenge worktop ('Wenge makes corian feel like formica,' he declares) and gazing into the camera as he holds aloft a coffee mug with 'snug' emblazoned across the front in Helvetica.

2   About decorated officers who were responsible for human rights abuses in postwar British colonies. After the 'eminent producer' pulled out, citing pressure from various British establishments, I turned to crowdfunding.

3   £22,683.

4   A Mr George Baggott, who lives in Stoke-on-Trent and pays a weasel called Vincent Hardy to manage his enormous property portfolio in the west of Scotland. Hardy's idea of managing property involves threatening tenants with violence, serving egregious eviction notices and ignoring emergency calls.

case, buying a flat had nothing to do with selfish aspiration or bourgeois materialism; no, we were casting off the manacles of tenancy once and for all. Not only that, we were buying an ex-rental that had been neglected for decades by another gluttonous, exploitative landlord. To stunned friends who could no doubt smell our guilt, we presented our diving into the property market almost as an act of self-sacrifice, as if we felt compelled to restore (we never used the term 'renovate') this piteous Victorian flat behind the library out of a sense of duty to our collective heritage. The stories we spin.

'It needs gutted,' we boasted to anyone who asked. 'Rewiring, replumbing, replastering, new kitchen, new bathroom, the lot.' We gave ourselves four months to get it to a habitable state, taking us right up to the end of our tenancy period. Nearly every weekend we would invite someone up to examine our work-in-progress, partly out of pride – it goes without saying that it was all being done tastefully and respectfully – and partly to illustrate just how much work we were putting into it, as if our labour somehow set us apart from anyone else who'd ever placed a foot on the first rung of the property ladder.

[NA: The foreground I've sketched here is far more detailed than I'd imagined, and with the 3000-word limit looming in the distance I've decided to skip the narrator's account of how Kyle abandoned his writing altogether in order to focus on the renovation and how he insisted on teaching himself plastering, plumbing and electrics by watching YouTube videos, while for the last couple of months she, our unnamed narrator, worked exhaustingly long hours on various shoots around England, culminating in a three-week stint inside an editing suite in London.]

So many words I have grown to hate as a consequence of our regular evening Facetime conversations. I'd be lying on some hotel bed in Norwich or Basingstoke or some other godforsaken place, listening to him drone on about mouldings and escutcheons and bulkheads and ingoes and ironmongery and sanitaryware and reclaimed this and reconditioned that. For a while these loathsome words became part of our shared lexicon, and though I knew they wouldn't be here for long – they were like verbal squatters – I hated them, never more so than when they leapt out of my own mouth, leaving their dirty footprints on my tongue.

[NA: The next few paragraphs digested: her resentment for him grows. As well as taking a sabbatical from writing, he confesses that he hasn't picked up a book for four months. He bores her with lists of deals he's picked up from Screwfix and Toolstation, and one night she almost passes out on her hotel bed as he relates in painful detail a confrontation he had that day with the intransigent manager of an independent paint shop on Argyle Street. Another time he induces a kind of nausea in her when he flashes his phone camera over his paint-streaked overalls. In short, his obsession with the flat starts to sicken her. Now, at last: the meat of the story.]

I came home most weekends, and it was on one such weekend, about a month before we were due to move in, that I discovered while sanding down the shelves in the hallway cupboard an undeveloped spool of film on the top shelf. That very afternoon I took it down to Snappy

Snaps on Byres Road, making it quite clear to the humourless android behind the counter that I'd found the spool in my new flat and whatever was on it had nothing to do with me. An hour later I picked up the photos, with nothing in the android's demeanor to suggest that anything extraordinary had been found on the celluloid. Rifling through the utterly mundane photos on the way back to the Hillhead flat I was beginning to lament the waste of the eight pounds it had cost me to develop them when, out of nowhere, after a sequence of six or seven shots of a red motorbike in someone's driveway, I struck gold. The first photo was of a twentyish guy lying on his back in bed – lean, short curls, coy smile – with both hands over his crotch. For a moment I thought I recognised him. The second was a close-up of his erect cock. And the next shot, a woman, naked, on the toilet, leaning forward, giggling, palm stretched out in a vain attempt to cover the lens. He'd surprised her. A post-coital joke, perhaps.

Kyle's reaction to the photos was so phlegmatic I retreated like an embarrassed schoolgirl. It was only later, when we entertained friends in our new kitchen and I would pull out the photos (rearranged so that the three explicit pictures were the last of the thirty-six), that Kyle tried to claim a share in my discovery. By then, of course, we'd made the link between the photos and the portfolio.

[NA: *What portfolio?* you might ask, and rightly so. An omission on my part, for which I can only apologise. Truth is, I can't be bothered making the onerous changes required to introduce the portfolio at the appropriate point in the narrative, so I'll settle on some exposition instead. On the February morning that our protagonists take the keys to their new flat, they discover in the walk-in cupboard of the main bedroom a large, black portfolio containing a dozen or so paintings and sketches, some of which contain the signature of a certain Donald Cowley in the bottom right-hand corner, and which are dated between 2006 and 2008. Of the work itself (bleak cityscapes, dark monoliths) our couple are intrigued rather than impressed, and if they consider framing and hanging a painting or two it's for sentimental reasons alone – to be able to say, 'These paintings are part of the history of the flat,' or some such sentiment. Anyway, on returning to their flat in Partick that same day, our narrator googles Donald Cowley to see if his paintings might be worth something. They're not: Donald Cowley now runs a construction company (remember footnote 1? God, I might have made all this so much clearer). And when, a few months later, our narrator is flicking through the photographs she's just had developed and thinks she recognises the guy with the erect cock, it's because that guy is Donald Cowley. Phew.]

I can't explain what prompted me to call Donald Cowley. We were at the second-coat-of-paint stage with the new flat, having sanded and sealed the floors and glossed all the woodwork. My contempt for Kyle was just starting to abate when, one Saturday night over a takeaway in our Partick flat, he declared a growing disillusionment with writing, making all sorts of spurious claims about the publishing industry and the Scottish literary scene as he prepared me for the news that he was going to renege on his contract with Finch Press, his publisher, and turn his hand to property development. He even had the temerity to compare himself to

Rimbaud, whom he described as a 'poet-turned-foreman'. I laughed so hard I had to spit my curry into a napkin. We then argued and he slept on the sofa for two nights, and it was on the Monday morning after the argument that I called Donald Cowley.

At his suggestion we met in a coffee shop on Crow Road. He arrived ten minutes late, pulling up on a Vespa and making a quick phone call before wandering in with a swagger. He was taller and chubbier than I'd expected and he looked a good ten years older than the man with the hard-on in the photos. Donald Cowley was not ageing gracefully. As I stood up to shake his hand my thigh caught the edge of the table, sending my coffee spilling all over his beige jeans. His mumbled response ('Fuck's sake') struck me as somewhat sinister and for a moment I wondered whether or not this was indeed the Donald Cowley of the cock and paintings. When he returned from the bathroom in his piebald jeans, he sat down, ordered a double espresso and produced an iPad from his bag. So, he began, you mentioned something about a TV series. Straight to the point. I explained that I was about to set up my own production company, and the first project I had in mind was a six-part series on Scottish businesses that were refreshing and revolutionizing their respective industries, and from what I'd seen and read snug fitted the bill perfectly. The flattery clearly lifted his spirits, so I went on. A good friend of mine at the BBC, a commissioner at Specialist Factual, was very keen on the idea, and as soon as I'd settled on my six businesses – narrowed down from a shortlist of eighteen – I was to meet her again to present my final proposal. So, tell me a little about yourself, I said. *If you want to be one of the six, impress me.* As he began to speak, his tone one of deep self-assurance, the sheer madness of what I had got myself into suddenly overwhelmed me and I missed the content of what he was saying. The urge came over me to toss the obscene photographs on the table (they were in my handbag on the floor) or castigate him for quitting art for commerce[5]. I wanted to ask him what had happened to the girl who'd taken his photo on the bed, the girl caught on the toilet. Was this it, then? Business, business, business? Was he at all disappointed in himself or did he find project managing middle-class people's home improvements creatively fulfilling? Did he still find time to read, to paint, to think?

[NA: I know, I know – I've made too explicit the parallels between Donald and Kyle, but there's no ignoring our narrator's sentiments as she listens inattentively to the voluble Cowley, tracking his gestures and mannerisms but registering none of his words. I should also make it clear that emotionally and psychologically, she has the self-awareness to understand her motives. She knows why she's sitting in a café with a man she knows only from various social media profiles, a handful of paintings and a photograph of his erect cock, and if she's feeling uncomfortable ('overwhelmed,' as she herself puts it) it's only because she doesn't know what it's all going to lead to or whether she'll lose her nerve and give the game away.]

I snatch the tail of something he says about designing his own range of dining chairs. My voice leaps out of my mouth almost of its own volition, and I find myself trailing after it, trying to reel it back in. Did you never consider being an artist? I mean professionally? Look,

5   According to his LinkedIn profile he'd graduated from the Glasgow School of Art in 2008, immediately going on to establish Cowley Furnishings Ltd. In 2010 he set up Cowley Ceramics Ltd, and in 2011 snug.

he says, I went to at art school under no illusions. The Scotia Nostra thing, that was history to me. It was already twenty years old. Does anyone I went to art school with make a living as an artist? Do they fuck – they're curators and wedding photographers. One of them's a cabinet maker, who I've got working for me, doing real work. He leans forward. See the ones who do make it as artists? Arseholes. Narcissists, every single one of them. By the way, he adds, I can tone it down for TV. Just be yourself, I say.

He picks up his iPad and for the next forty-five minutes he talks me through slideshow after slideshow of extensions, attic conversions, wetroom installations, office refurbishments and landscaping projects. There is nothing that snug don't do, and do better than anyone else. They don't employ tradesmen; they employ craftsmen. And their craftsmen also happen to be gentlemen. He likes to describe snug as a collective of artists and artisans transforming the 'landscape that people inhabit.' It's more than just excellence and expertise they have to offer – it's an ethos, a philosophy, a *relationship*. The construction industry, as Cowley sees it, has for far too long regarded itself as exempt from contemporary business practices, and snug intends to change that. Before Cowley gets up to leave (he has a prospective client to see in Jordanhill – reroofing) he tosses a pamphlet and some flyers onto the table.

Two weeks later he calls me. It's a Friday and I'm having lunch at my desk and when his number appears on my phone I slide it to mute. In the message he refers to himself as Don[6] and he sounds out of breath. I can hear seagulls squawking in the background. The image of his erect cock flashes before me, and that of the girl on the toilet, and the sight of my sandwich induces a nausea that stays with me for the rest of the day.

I'll get around to calling him back on Monday or Tuesday. I'll say something about budget cuts at the BBC; and that, I expect, will be that. Meanwhile, I put a reminder on my phone for the following morning: 'bin pics and photos.'

[NA: An unsatisfactory ending. I had intended something else, but an artist friend of mine put me off by describing it as 'misogynistic shite.' I suspect he'll consider this to be just as misogynistic and shite, but it's the best I can do. Before I wrap things up, I'd also like to add that it didn't take long for Kyle, our narrator's boyfriend/husband/lover, to rediscover his ability to read without distraction, and the writing soon followed. He never again expressed a desire to do anything other than write for a living. All in all, a happy ending. Of sorts.]

(3,000 words on the dot – including this one).

---

6   The message in full: 'Hi, it's Don. Just following up on our recent meeting about your series on entrepreneurs. We've just won a fabulous contract to convert an old schoolhouse in Stranraer into a maritime museum and I thought it would be the perfect thing for you. You'll get to see how the whole process works, from the initial design to the grand opening. I guess you'll want to start filming a.s.a.p. and I can slow things up my end until you're ready to shoot. Call me.'

From The Atlas Mountains, with Love

David Crystal

In the cave of nothingness
the hunted animals escape from their feeble
painting and kill their hunters.
I slip past the night porter
with wine, vodka and salted almonds,
Google her name, horse behaviourist, dancer
the first patient to undergo a bloodless transplant.
I remember her aversion to hot drinks
her flat in Manor House invaded by rats.
Never looking crossing busy Camden roads
late always for everything.

Professor Karimo

David Crystal

I will fuck the devil out of you
I will save family from drugs and crime
I will cure dogs of bad odours
I will give you spells to bring back happiness.

I have magic dust to make money come
I am the Professor of good things.

I have eyes that will help you see again
Make the song you sing different
Forever protect you from bad neighbours.

No Life without problems.
No Problems without solution.

One Crutch Danny

David Crystal

Takes his crutch out for a stroll
every day. He holds the crutch horizontally.
The crutch wants to do its job
but is not allowed. The crutch is no substitute for a dog
and not that much of a catch as a crutch.
Occasionally used as a weapon, the crutch enjoys
scuffles outside ISTANBUL, our 24 hr liquor store.
Once in the Persian Deli, the crutch was used
to pin down a lizard, as Danny talked to a local
preacher, who wore a necklace of teeth,
teeth that he picked out of a ceiling
just before the Feds and the forensic teams arrived.

6-4-1

David Crystal

A tricast for Saïd, at the Stade Velodrome, Casablanca.
He shows me a rusty old key, a dream key for the great Riad
(flattened to make way for a souk, selling mobile phone paraphernalia).
On a gold chaise longue, a greyhound with the greenest eyes, sleeps.
Saïd steals the dog, wins four big races on the trot. A dream
like walking over cool marble, past a courtyard fountain
to feast on quail and lamb tagine with relatives long dead.
One day he will find the right money for the Shisha shop
lost in a Poker game after too much wine.
On the bus to El Jadida, a cloud of white Ibis
fly at truck height. A man with a hawk's head
hands me a brown pebble, looks to the field of rocks and stones
solitary figures in the twilight, bending towards the earth.

Borges' Paradox

Sean Martin

– We create our own forebears

We each carry that secret leech-book,
places linked to us
in gazetteers of pain and wonder,

a finger-thin bone of coast
in some brine-drenched rutter,
a cortex of leys:

Newcraighall.
North Tawton.
The road to Thurso.

The Girl Who Got Onto the Ferry in *Citizen Kane*

Sean Martin

Everett Sloane recalls the girl in white he saw,
back in '96, stepping off the Jersey ferry.
She didn't see him, but he's thought of her each day since:

everything's in slow-mo, chestnut hair
bunched beneath her hat, one ringlet
falling across her face like an ear of tall grass;

her parasol paints her face with shade.
Now she's crossing a street in Prague
unaware she's on that ferry, Manhattan's shadow

on her like a hand. Or she's coming out
of the metro at Gamla Stan, Nordic tresses
queenly, or buying flowers on Rue Beautreillis,

and disappearing from view
into a cobbled yard full of sheets and cats.
She was never there. The film loops over and over.

The Moon: Three Poems
(one sonnet, one tanka, one haiku)

Alan Spence

MOONSONG

The moon is opening her mouth to sing.
She makes no sound, her song is made of light,
a song so lucid, cool, I feel it ring
in every cell, make me shine loud, sing bright.
Drunk on moonshine, I'm lunatic, pure mad.
The clear light of her singing fills my brain,
wells up inside my heart and makes me glad.
Its sweet intoxication drives me sane.
I'm in this moment, in this place, this time,
but here and now I know I'm limitless.
The night's a silver bell, I feel it chime –
illumination-song in emptiness.
Across a quarter million miles of space
I smile back at my original face.

A hundred miles north,
I know you're looking at
the same moon –
thinking of me as
I'm thinking of you.

broken again
whole again
moon in the water

Landscape With Figures
(An Idyll)

Jim C Wilson

I painted my sky Greek-island blue;
hills, rug-soft, were Wordsworth green.
My river, brimming with sky, tumbled gently,
then meandered out of the frame.
(The bathing was perfect.)
Gods and goddesses languished in silk,
their hair fair and softly curling.
Doric temples, precisely positioned,
were white as the skin of maidens.
Wild roses with red satin petals
mingled with daisies which sparkled.
I tried to add a unicorn, shining
in a July dawn. But my colours ran,
perspectives changed,
and the brush grew a thorn.

That emptiness subsides,
but don't kid yourself.
Ten, fifteen years later,
when it chooses to, the
emptiness will still rise
up and crush you.

Late
Kevin MacNeil

Late

Kevin MacNeil

The girl at the bus stop grinned hard, tilted her head and slipped her tingling hand into mine and softly tugged me onto the number 33. It was late. I felt like she needed to tell me something. As Rome's sparkling lights glided past, there were these terrific frissons and we talked about the shows we'd seen, where our weird accents were from, how gorgeously the full August moon glowed, how equally stunning her face looked (I said this, and she didn't disagree, she carried on smiling as though a kitten were kissing at her toes) and then, when leaning in, whisper-exclaiming something about the moon, her lips almost touched my ear and I had full-body goosebumps.

The bus pulled up alongside a hotel – my hotel, I realised with a happy frown. The journey had been so fast and smooth I felt limousined there, and on alighting I thanked the driver and checked my hand when it reached into a pocket in search of a tip.

There was no one at reception.

'What's our room number?' she said as we climbed the lavish staircase. My arm had found its home in hers.

I fished in my pocket again, this time producing a keycard, and I handed it over. She beamed and guided me to the door. I felt like she still needed to tell me something but maybe she'd temporarily changed her mind. The room was large, gently lit, the bed plush and easy and warm and breathless and needy and animalistic and harmonise-y and ecstatic. We sank down, smiling, into exhausted sleep with such a synchronising of breath I half-imagined we would share the same dream, maybe something about twins swimming in tandem, streaming breaststroke through the night sky like a whole new emotion.

Morning opened like a Japanese novel and I wanted to tell her so, using words like understated, askew, natural, perfect. But she was gone from bed.

'Morning,' she said, startling me. I turned. She stood sober, collected, already dressed, handing me a glass. 'Got you some grapefruit juice.'

I sipped, tasted blood. 'What's wrong?' I said.

She laughed. 'Drink it all down.'

I did. 'Wait – you're leaving?'

'I gotta be somewhere.'

'You are somewhere.'

'It's nine fifteen. I'm already late.'

'You can't leave. I'm going to kidnap you.' The way I said it just didn't sound right.

She glanced at a wall, looked at her watch, analysed briefly a fingernail. Her black hair swayed heavy where it was still a little damp. She wore no make-up. Somewhere a clock ticked, moving us forward.

'You are every bit as beautiful without make-up.'

She brightened for a moment as though seeing herself in my mind, the way I saw her. I pulled her close, pressed a hot slow meaningful kiss onto the back of her hand.

'Silly,' she said. 'I gotta go. I'm so late. I'm going. No. Seriously.' I felt like there was something she couldn't tell me.

'Call me?' I said. She let me give her my number. I also traced the words 'Tell me' onto her thigh with my finger, a secret gesture, a pact.

What I wanted was to have her undress, slide back into bed with me, let me hug her and kiss her and praise her and listen to her for the rest of the day. (I was to spend two decades composing inscrutable poems on her smiling beauty, only to burn all of them, inadequate.)

I know myself, know that if someone, something, offered to give me the rest of that day with her in exchange for, say, cutting my life short by ten or fifteen years, I would have signed my blood away and thanked him, it. The power to make someone feel complete or empty is terrible.

Anyway, she left.

I lay there, brimful with a kind of ongoing mental hunger, a craving – an emptiness that hurts, even though it's as empty as what you can't remember from before you were born.

That emptiness subsides, but don't kid yourself. Ten, fifteen years later, when it chooses to, the emptiness will still rise up and crush you. Rome is half a world away and she – she is altogether further away than that. I am no longer me. Time grows slowly, reveals itself to be made of bone. The moon is an inhospitable hunk of rock. In real life no one smiles as hard as a skull does, that should tell us all something.

The Last Makar

David Forrest

The last makar didna actually ken the leid himsel. The man wis a dumm, but nae deif like the lave. He'd hearken to it, fand the wirds, follae the seentences hame. A docky pit doon, a mad maument o flytin, an amour. See, the leid cam oot ae aw o us whan we meent whit we said. Whin we didna ken oorsels, thon auncient leid aye kent. The makar clarkit doon for aw ae us. Gowden groff-write.

Baurm the politeecian! Baurm the keeng! Bairn efter bairn efter bairn kent the soon ae seelence, the soon ae jis waitin for end. Haudin the needle in. Sayin oor last goodbye, then saying nothing.

Castles. Dykes. A rickle o stanes. Yon man could hear. An when aw becam seelence, the leid becam aw. Coudna hush it, coudna stap, the man wis leid – nae faimly, nae job, jis this streenge muisic, pushin him alang, makin him write, makin him cant. He could scrieve a wird tae scrieve a man.

But he couldna mak fuid an he couldna mak susteenance, his ain leid wid malkie him afore lang.

Threescore an ten, an then a leid is dun.

Ither makars could mak a leevin fae sassanach wi slevvers ae Scots. It wisna Scots, nae mair than tatties are saut.

Threescore and ten, and then a leed is done.

The makar deed but the wirds didna stap. The lingert on his grave an are hauntin him still. 'Bonnie. Eyedent. Misst.'

He wis the youngest o wummin or the auldest a men or he's whitever mishanter that brings it aw hame...

He wis his ain man. He wis his ain man.

Circle Stone

Simon Sylvester

I walked along the high street, endlessly replaying the breakdown of my last relationship. I was startled from my melancholy by a man selling avocados.

'Three for a quid. And for you, sweetheart,' he winked, 'I'll chuck in a dream for free.'

I went home, sliced the avocados, and ate them with lemon juice, salt and pepper.

Sure enough, that night, I had a dream. It was round, and it was perfect.

I dreamed of avocados.

Seein's Believin

Ethyl M Smith

It wis a cauld nicht, wi the win souchin roond the ootside o the yurt. In by we wur snug as a bug. Twelve o us in oor thick, woolly plaids, lien in a roond, wi oor feet pintin tae the middle whaur a wee, black stove wis cracklin awa.

We micht hae lukt as if we wur sleepin, or jist toastin oor taes. Bit naw. We wur poised on the cusp o a journey, so huvin a snooze wis the last thing on oor mind. Wud be shamans so we wur, wi a wheen lessons unner oor belt. Noo it wis time tae step intae the ether an meet oor totem animal. Each tae thur ain madness ah suppose, an we wur keen tae dae whitever wis needit.

The maister hud tellt us we aw hae ane, even if we didna ken. We jist hud tae follae the soond o the drum an slide intae middle earth, whaurever that micht be, fur thaim as ken say it's heavin wi totem animals, aw waitin fur the likes o us tae cam by.

The maister liftit his drum, a bittie reindeer skin streetched ower a roond frame, an hit it wi a lang bane. Thur wis a saft boom. The sign fur oor lift aff. Anither boom, than anither, cannie yit reglar till it got intae a rhythm, an intae oor heid. Kinda mesmerisin, an allooin the imagination tae tak ower.

The boom o the drum wis workin fur me. In nae time ah'm wis in amang a swurlin mist, slidin intae middle earth as if sittin on a lang watter shute in a pleisure park. It wisna scary, an ah wisna fashed. Aw ah wantit wis that furst sicht o ma vera ain totem animal.

Than it happened. A daurk shape cam oot o the swurlin trails. It luked lik some kinda burd, an ma een wur oot on stalks hopin tae mak oot a symbolic an meaninfu craitur lik an aigle, or a falcon, or even a peacock.

Whan ah did mak it oot ah wis gobsmacked fur therr it wis, yella as a sunflooer, a dancin, prancin, yella budgie. No whit ah wis aifter at aw.

Mind ye it wis a takin kinda burd, an ah hud tae smile, fur nixt thing it staunds on its heid, waves its claws aboot, an gies ane or twa squawks. An ah cud hae sweered it winked at me afore richtin itsel. Aifter that it sterts runnin back an furrit, flappin its wings, noddin its heid, bowin an scrapin, swingin this way an that afore the finale whan it cam up close, turns its wulkies lik a circus clown, than vanishes intae the mirk.

It didna cam back. An ah wisna sorry fur whae wants a yella budgie as thur totem animal?

Ah kept on starin, an hopin, bit saw nuthin till the drum beat chainged an tellt me ma time wis up. Ah wis oot o luck. Bit nae maitter, ah whizzed back frae middle earth, intae the yurt agane, an sat up tae rub ma een.

We aw bid quate fur a wheen meenits, gaitherin oor richt senses. An than the maister pits a lang, white feather in the midst o the flair. He bows tae us an says, 'When you feel moved to speak reach in, take this feather, then share your experience. You may speak for as long or as little as you choose.'

Ye must be jokin ah thocht. Bit naw. Richt awa ane o the group taks haud o the feather an launches intae meetin a tiger, hoo its message wis aw aboot bravery, an bein special, an god kens whit else afore he pit the feather back. Aifter that anither ane lifts it tae tell us aboot a muckle elephant, bringin him strength, an advisin him tae mind the things that maitter an deefie the tittle tattle. On an on it went, awbody waxin eloquent, wantin tae share thur special beastie.

Did ah feel an eedjit? Did ah no. So ah jist bid stoom fur aw ah hud wis a daft, wee, yella budgie. Ah didna even luk at the feather let alane mak a move fur it.

An than the maister catches ma ee. 'Please. Will you share?'

'Naw,' ah whuspered, an shuk ma heid,

An he jist smirks an pints at the feather.

Weel ah did try tae defy him, an ah didna move fur a guid meenit. Bit whit wi him smirkin, an pintin, an aw the rest starin, ah fin masel crawlin furrit tae lift yon feather.

Bit afore ah stertit ma speil ah tellt thaim braw plain, 'Ah'm no wantin tae dae this fur ye'll jist laugh.'

That did it. Ye cud hae heard a peen drap. No a cheep.

Aifter that thur wis nae way back so ah pued masel thegither an stertit on aboot ma wee, yella clown. An it wisna sae bad. Aifter a meenit ah cud see they wur listenin. In fact they wur leanin furrit, interestit like. An the mair ah said the mair it seemed richt.

An they did laugh.

An so did ah, fur clair as day, ah cud see thon burd wisna daft. It wis richt lang heidit. Its antics hud been tellin me tae lichten up, an stoap bein sae faur up masel. An hearin the ithers laugh jist confirmed it.

Ye see, meetin ma wee, yella budgie jist gied me whit ah needit, an shawed me hoo guid common sense can pop up in mony a disguise. An aften when we least expeck it.

Archaeology

Richard W Strachan

First layer

We always see abandoned things through the eyes of a witness, a survivor or an explorer, and not as they should be; unpeopled, devoid of a single human presence.

There was no one waiting to meet me when I arrived. I came out onto a wide, unmarked street. The city was deserted.

There were cars parked by the side of the road. In the carelessness of their angles against the pavement, the way a wheel mounted the kerb, was the suggestion that they had been left there permanently. No one would be coming back to fit the keys to the locks and spark the engines into life. The buildings on either side of the road were quiet too, not with a temporary sense of vacancy but with the imperishable silence of something forever abandoned. As I walked on I had the sense that the people here had just downed tools and, as if compelled to fulfill some long-dormant instinct or a migratory pattern that they didn't fully understand, had moved *en masse* towards more peaceful and fertile habitats. I imagined a column of figures streaming from the canyons of the streets, no belongings but the clothes they wore, their gestures gradually loosening and becoming more relaxed the further they got into the surrounding countryside, their faces brightening perhaps, and the tense and locked-down expressions smoothing out into an openness that matched the wide country around them. Behind them, sullen and silent, was the city; discarded, like an experiment that had gone badly wrong, none of it worth salvaging. In the absence of people came the colonising dust, the gritty layering of sand that crunched underfoot as I headed deeper into the streets, stepping on the first green shoots of the weeds that would eventually engulf them.

Second layer

I gathered a firmer image of the city as I walked through it, crossing the grids, noting the details and idiosyncrasies of each quarter. After walking for thirty minutes or so I came to a spread of parkland, and in the centre I saw a lake ringed by a walkway. There were ducks and moorhens gliding with vacant expectancy across the water. On one side of the lake there were half a dozen small huts, wattle and daub constructions, huddled together as if seeking warmth from each other. I knew without stepping inside them that they would all be empty. Leaning into the dim doorways I could smell old sweat, the musky reek of unwashed bodies and animal skins, and the sweet fragrance of stale woodsmoke. At the centre of the group of huts there was a scorched patch of ground, the brittle charcoal of burned wood, ash, bone.

From somewhere on the other side of the park I was sure I could hear a car's engine, grinding upwards through its gears, hitting a high whine that soon faded into the low zone of my tinnitus. I paused on the grass, head tilted up to look up at the white-streaked sky, the cold sun.

There was something else as well, apprehended, felt rather than glimpsed; like an encroaching shadow, leaking very slowly from the direction in which I had come. I tried not to look back.

As I left the huts behind, another movement caught my eye. I saw two figures moving hurriedly off through the further gate. They were too far away to tell if they were male or female, young or particularly old, but I felt curiously deflated at the sight of them, my fantasy of complete depopulation reduced now to more manageable and realistic proportions. I called after the figures but they didn't answer. Did one of them stop, shocked at the intrusion into their own fantasy of silence? Did he or she look back wildly for the source of this unforeseen shout, the evidence of another man in a world they thought was their kingdom alone? They were too far away now, I couldn't tell. Possibly they had. But it was equally possible that they had not.

I had only been walking for two or three miles, but soon began to feel tired. I was thirsty, hungry; I couldn't remember when I had last had anything to eat or drink, and as soon as the idea was present in my mind I felt an almost uncontrollable thirst. There were no shops on the street, no food stalls on the walkways that I could see, and in any case I didn't seem to have any money on me. I had nothing on me but my clothes, and even in my clothes I felt suddenly naked, unprotected. I crouched down by the water, in the shadow of the mud huts, and even though I knew there was no one watching me I still looked around like an animal at a watering hole before palming up a drink.

Satisfied for the moment, I sat down on a bench and closed my eyes. Looking into that interior darkness, I concentrated on the range of sounds that moved through the empty city, the moaning wind as it skirted the buildings, the ruffled gasp of the leaves and the grass, and the water cuffing lightly against the banks of the lake.

When I opened my eyes I felt that there had been some shift in the atmosphere, a lowering of the sky's lid, and the cloud cover was somehow deeper and more resistant to the breeze. The light was blunt, and in the lee of the benches opposite me I saw the angle of a shadow beginning to thicken. I glanced nervously towards the gate where I had entered the park, but there was nothing there. And now this shadow, this darkness, thickening and becoming more pronounced, as if it was reaching out towards me.

I stood up to leave, walking around the circumference of the lake towards the streets on the other side of the park, where the rest of the city was laid out like a chessboard. I saw a discarded newspaper flapping in the breeze on one of the benches and picked it up, scanning the pages to see if I could get some idea of where I was, and when. The I stopped and sat down, and read the story that had caught my eye from start to finish.

It was a follow-up feature about an archaeological dig on the city's northern outskirts. A housing development, I read, where work had been suspended after the discovery of human remains. There in the mud, scraped clean by the first probing sweep of a digger's toothed bucket, had been a small knuckle of bone, unrecognisable to the layman but, to the young archaeologist who had held the watching brief on the project, the first sign of an extraordinary discovery.

It had been the skeleton of an adult male, a neolithic hunter. He had been buried with deliberation, and his grave goods – weapons, pots, beads – were remarkably well preserved. With great effort and skill the archaeologists had scraped away a millimetre at a time the accreted dirt of ten thousand years, and when the bones were finally disinterred they were taken to the university for further study. Now, at last, the repaired figure was going on display at the museum, and alongside the skeleton was a specially-commissioned facial reconstruction of this ancient ancestor, based on a minute and highly detailed osteological examination of the cranial remains. In gazing on this ancient man, people would be given the chance to gaze vertiginously into the unimaginable past, to look upon some haunting genetic echo of themselves and wonder at the gaudy fabric of his cosmos, his culture, his incomprehensible view of the patterned world around him.

All this in itself would be of great interest, enough to stop anyone in their tracks. But this was not what had given me pause. What had made me grip the sheets in my hands and find the nearest seat was not the story itself, but the picture of the face that accompanied it, that reconstruction of the ancient dead man. There in the pages of the newspaper, staring at me across those ten thousand years, was my own face; unmistakable, exact, and frighteningly calm.

Third layer

The museum was what I would have expected, a frontage of pastiche classicism with colonnades and pillars and a dome transposed from the skyline of ancient Rome. I had followed my instincts to find it, tracing what I felt were the buried patterns of any city of comparable size. As I walked, I saw little evidence of other people on the streets. A slammed window, a scuffling tread of footsteps disappearing around a dusty corner. Fleet figures moved sometimes in the distance, and over everything came the ragged, windswept progress of crumpled paper, rubbish, dead leaves. And, always somehow out of sight, yet still creeping closer to me, was this sense of a shadow moving from the edge of the city, unfurling from where I had arrived and reaching a thick tendril down all the wide and narrow streets towards me, wherever I was.

From the double doors came a woman and her two children, drifting down the steps and getting into a car that was parked haphazardly at the side of the road. Inside, I saw other people, strolling casually through the atrium and disappearing into the gallery ahead. Here then was where the few people who remained here had chosen to go. Perhaps the figures I had seen on the other side of the park had been rushing here, eager to catch a glimpse of the new display – perhaps this was some necessary ritual before abandoning the city for good? The dead ancestor must be appeased before the old hunting grounds are given up, lest his spirit wander for eternity seeking the camp fires and the reeking feasts of a tribe that is no longer there.

I saw more people wandering in small groups of twos and threes, sometimes people on their own, all glancing at the display cabinets as if rehearsing the future observations that others would make of their own cast-off detritus, relics made significant only by the passage of time. They wandered obliquely, choosing displays at random, pausing only to give each assemblage the most cursory examination before walking off deeper into the museum complex. They were all heading in the same direction, and without stopping at any of the other exhibits I followed them into the heart of the building, where the neolithic hunter was laid out under a soft amber light. He lay in his coffin of glass, a swatch of brown bones watched over by a clay and wax impression of my own impassive countenance.

It was unmistakably my own face, gazing down in the modelling clay and plastic of the forensic anthropologist's art. The hair was different, an unruly matted wig, and the skin colour, to give the semblance of a life lived out of doors was a shade or two darker than my own, but everything else gave me the wrenching impression of looking into a three-dimensional mirror, or as if I had confronted a previously-unsuspected identical twin. I disguised my reaction from anyone who might have been watching, and to an observer I must have seemed no more than mildly interested in the exhibition. Inside though, I was choking with shock. I felt displaced – literally displaced, moved from where I was standing to some point beyond myself, beyond the cool, low-lit museum hall, into the moulding of the life-size bust mounted on its metal stick, with its fringed cloak of buckskin and hide.

When a space became clear, the others eventually moving away and wandering back the way they had come, I leaned in closer to the display cabinet for a better look at the bones themselves. I stared down at the grave goods. Flint blades as long as my hand, arrowheads, plates and bowls that looked as if they had been roughly carved from ivory. There were handfuls of animal teeth, holes bored at the roots where they had obviously been strung together. The twine had rotted to nothing thousands of years before. None of it had any intrinsic value, and the workmanship was, with the best will in the world, crude. What vigour these items possessed came from their immense age and, more than anything, from their utility, the sense they radiated of long and reliable use; for what hunter would be sent into the afterlife with goods that he could not in the waking world rely upon to serve him well?

The longer I stayed there, the more fascinated I became by these grave goods. I looked at them, artfully arranged on either side of the skeleton's fragmented skull, and imagined them in their proper state. What would each arrow feel like knocked to the string of its bow? How would the spear balance itself to the throwing arm, with the long, murderous flint aimed at the flank of an animal? I felt I knew. I could feel that weight in my arm just by looking at it, I could feel the tension in the wire of the bow string as I pulled it back and let the arrow fly. I knew all this just by looking.

I came out of my trance, glancing up from the glass surface of the cabinet to realise that I was once again alone. The museum was empty, and the lights had been turned down low. I saw the pale green glow of the emergency light above the fire door wink once and stop, but then from elsewhere in the museum, washing slowly through its corridors and exhibition spaces like a tide of molasses, came that feeling of darkness, flowing not from a single place now but from what felt like every corner of the city at once. This time I knew that if I stood still it would engulf me.

It took me only moments to break the glass of the cabinet roof. I gathered up the relics, slipping the beads, the animal teeth, the arrowheads into my pockets. I took up the blade and held it like a dagger, and in the other hand I held the cup of bone. I had to have these things. They were mine. They would protect me.

I started to run, and the waves of darkness flexed away from me, only to swell back and cover my every line of retreat, funneling me into one particular direction. From the museum I found myself heading into the city streets, tunnels of dust that soon opened out into wide, clean avenues strobed by flat white light. Growing above me on either side were vast structures of chrome and steel. I was running through a glass canyon, my footsteps scattering into echoes, each geometrically precise plane of the buildings showing me the unvarying stare of the streetlights, the cold glow of harnessed noble gases and sodium vapour. And the lights lost their inert vigour, pulsing down into darkness, and I was following the line that I was allowed to take from those glacial streets towards the north, into the hills, into the sudden woods that sprung up around me, and when I looked back between the pillars of the trees, the tall gods of the green spaces and the smudged shadows of the ferns, I could see the hostile campfires of the settlement winking, brands taken by the strangers from the flame and carried up into the hills after me, stone hunter straying from the pathways of my gods. I run on, sheathed in leather, pine crushed underfoot and whipping branches striking me. The huts are burning now, arrows are leaping from the dark –

Then darkness holds me, a stone, plunging me into the mud and pine, the blanket of the undergrowth, into the black stars. The dead moon, the wide sea of silver rivers, and the endless meadows underground...

Fourth layer

They were all so eager when the call was made, though disguising it with their professionalism, as if it would be unseemly to rush with such excitement towards the dead.

When they disinterred his skull, flecking the earth from the occipital bones, there may have been some among them who would have felt themselves capable of sinking down into an imaginative reconstruction of his life (like sinking into the hard and at first unyielding water of a hot bath), but no one there could possibly have understood the real range of his distress as he stumbled down to die, or fully imagine the tide of blood that deafened him and dragged him under. None could have understood how or if in the moment of his death he would have slotted the experience into the broad and self-replenishing helix of his culture, calling on any number of unguessable gods, the spirits that leisurely animated the grass and quickened the beasts or flocked the thunderclouds in menacing array around the buttresses of distant mountains. They could have tried, the archaeologists, but no matter how much they were educating their guesses with the patiently acquired information of their studies, the images and sequences and ideas they conjured up would always have been at least partly a projection of their own interests and desires, the dissatisfactions that they may have felt, stranded in the depths of their own culture; as pervasive and inescapable as the pantheon of corn gods or chthonic deities that the dead skull would have gazed upon with full acceptance and understanding in the days when it still wore its mask of flesh, and was alive. Else, why disinter the past in the first place, if not feeling that it went in some way towards explaining or excusing your present?

So the skull gazed hollowly from the earth as they worked, and they gave it their tender attention, patiently loving these old and resurrected bones. Then, when they had finished, they brought the bones out and carried them off, to be repaired, rearranged, reimagined, and I found myself once more forgetting, standing out on a wide avenue ringed with dust, and the city all abandoned around me.

The details

Judith Taylor

He keeps his paperwork resolutely
up-to-date: works on some nights
till it's finished. For it's so easy
to lose your grip on the details
then to be asked to account for something and
have to scrabble for it. None of that

in his department. Everything's logged:
arrivals, assets, relevant correspondence
and disposals, all
clearly filed. He can lay his hand
on anything you might want to know, in a second.
And he flatters himself

the smooth way the process runs out there
reflects the orderly way it's documented.
That's his contribution.
Calm and order
spreading outwards from his filing-room
like light.

      No, that's too grand:
but like a benign contagion, maybe,
making better the world. He thinks himself
– will go to his grave
thinking himself – a cog, yes,
but a vital one in the great machine.

He will go to his grave
resolutely
thinking he was a good man
and all he did was his duty.

The Symbolists

Judith Taylor

(after graphic works by Edvard Munch,
Scottish National Gallery of Modern Art, August 2012)

It was your friend who called her *Vampire*
and the name stuck.
You thought of him as your friend still

though he's the one who looks at you, his face
bleak as death, from every version you made of *Jealousy*

and you're the man in the background
with his wife, in conversation
under the apple-tree in the garden.

You came to regret it later
- the name, that is.
It took all ambiguity from the picture

and in fact it's just a woman
kissing a man on the neck, you said.

But it was you who gave her red hair
when you printed the colour series.

Manifesto

Judith Taylor

Poetry is an art where
   not enough
                is rude and unpleasant; but
       in her what is beautiful
is not: whence   a poet ought to chuse

(by erasure from POETRY, in the first edition of the <u>Encyclopaedia Britannica</u>, 1768-71)

Pennies, or how I single handedly got us out of the crisis

Juana Adcock

When I arrived to the so-called united
kingdom reigned by automatons and charlatans my money
soon ran out. I found in the pantry
of the humble hostel that housed me a big jarfull
of brown penny conserve, organic and handmade in a farm in the north of France.
From that vital jelly I started stealing, a bit at a time,
to buy a pint of milk, any bread.
I rummaged too
through bins for dispersed spaghetti strands,
for peppers almost rotting.
Often in my last moments of hope
I found in a puddle a heavy pound coin
then I invested it all at once
an offering from the god of money to the god of cacao.
I stole the apples fallen to the pavement
I stole plastic rings from pound shops
I rose at dawn to slave at the till,
the coins that fell as I cashed up
stapling through my temples with their high-pitched
smell of gunshots in lands of other men stolen by other men.
It's not mine, it's not mine, it's not mine, it's not mine, it's not yours, it's not theirs, it's
not ours.

How many times did I walk for hours for lacking
the last missing penny for my bus fare.
But one day I cracked it: I remembered the jar of conserve, always full, no matter how
much I stole.

What we needed was to plant pennies on the pavement
to gift ourselves a feeling of abundance—a penny a day
keeps your bad luck away. The sole
speculation magical intention
that transforms self-referencing Money
into self-referencing money. The god of money is circular:

may it not stagnate, may it—meagre as milk—never run out
just like cows when they pour themselves out
or that clear
whisky first currency of Scotland
uisge beatha first water of life
pissed out of a cow

Closing Monostiches

Lindsay Macgregor

Rookery
Bickering again about black ribbon, obsidian canopic jars, stolen camphor

Translation of Ibsen's note to self concerning remedy for venereal disease
The pharmacy selling mercury is in the wooden house at the foot of Storgaten by the Skagerakk.

Hesiod's Last List
Alexandro's honey, three strings of peppers, cured meats from Crete, two kilos sweetest barrel wine

High Foss in Winter
Rigor mortis gripping water hard against the pall of blackened rock.

The Morrigan
Already she's washing blood from your clothes at the midnight crossroads

Riddle
Who tore out both her eyes and skewered them on a sharpened aspen twig near Restalrig?

Not there yet
This is as far as I can go.

Reality Check
I (seem to) see a ghost

Live Well
Waste time wisely

Quotidian heroics
Daylight saving time

Think before you
Too late

Fire's Constant Question
What good would burning do?

Reply
Learn to live without an answer

Out of Body Experience
Most souls are dying for one

After Life
You might as well whistle to the other world

Emily

Kay Ritchie

(i.m. Emily Davison Wilding – 1872-1913)

they prepared you well
incarcerated 9 times
made to do hard labour
your cell filled with ice cold water and
forced to gorge like duck or goose
being finished for the slaughter

on 49 occasions
a naso gastric tube fed through nose to stomach via oesophagus
spread disease made you bleed lungs fit to bust
like African girls whose mothers perform gavage

they're off
a flat sprint
jockeys wild in silks
past the bushes
race-goers on car roofs in top hats
boaters feathers plumes caps
and 3rd from last
almost past Tattenham corner
Herbert Jones on Anmer

from beneath the rail
a suffragette scarf flaps
as you bolt free towards
the king's own horse
full of run
your final battle cry
VOTES FOR WOMEN
then like a stone once thrown at
David Lloyd George
you drop
inside the bend of Epsom's horseshoe

unlucky for you
hair now spread across the mud
flame red as those pillar boxes once set alight

your face now pallid WHITE
your bruises vivid PURPLE
your GREEN eyes closed against the light
never to know how
you advanced our fight.

My Dresses Appear in Markets

Kathrine Sowerby

I wash my naked body in cooking water, morning and night, trickle gold urine
behind shutters in my freezing hut while, swinging like lanterns in alpine winds,
my clothes are auctioned, garment by loose-fitting garment.

A stand selling kidneys and asparagus grilled over hardwood embers and oil
hangs its smell in my jackets and shirts. Sparrows nest in my bell-shaped sleeves,
shoulder to shoulder: hinges d'amour.

I've thrown it all away: rectangles sewn to triangles, buttons fastened to cuffs
like flattened berries. Dresses smocked and feathered at the waist, leave me now,
glazed in layers of sweat and something resembling air.

Compline

Tracey S Rosenberg

I pray throughout the evening. With perfect stitches
I mend your cloak, closing the rents in its frayed shoulders
with silver thread. I cooked this soup with such care;
now I pour it, spiced and hot, into your flask.
Everything you need must fit in your bag. It is easy to pray
when my hands are full of missals, herbs, sandals.
I listen for splashings as you wash and dress.
Here are your sturdy boots; I waxed them again
to protect your feet against the endless rain.

When you enter the hall, I am seated beside your bag,
biting off a final thread. My heart laughs
at your boyish wet hair. You are brisk but not unkind.
As you shrug into your cloak
without waiting for my hands to help,
you announce that so much work awaits you in the world.
Thousands of souls are plunging into joyful damnation.
The poor misguideds reject the divine,
too busy with the work of this world
and its heretical passions, their beastly souls
blazing with secondary heat!

Striding towards the door
you give your final orders
for the coming months.
Your cloak twists, caught up in itself.
I am reaching out, praying, lips tight.
As you cross the threshold,
I lean forward under the frozen stars
and pull your cloak straight.
Within my hands, the silver threads hold fast.

War bird

Carol McKay

A collared dove
in a bomb-blown tree
masquerades
as a carrier bag.

Grubby white
it's a towel hung
in a kitchen too long.

A flag of truce,
dirtied, overlooked.

But Earth's axis whirs;
stirred, bird
stretches one wing,

chameleon against the sky
and the ground's cold crust.

For a moment she thought about adding him to her tattooed men collection. Sensitive Marshall who had 'meet is murder' across his thin, blue-white chest. Too sensitive to tell the tattoo girl that she'd spelled it wrong.

The Last Big Weekend of the Summer
Margaret Callaghan

Extract from the novel
The Last Big Weekend of the Summer

Margaret Callaghan

The barman leaned over the bar and handed her a tequila.

'That one's on me,' he yelled above the four different baseball games blaring out of each of the televisions above his head. 'My great-grandparents are from Scotland.'

'Where from?' she yelled back, carefully floating the tequila on her beer as Jesse had taught her, squeezing the lime on top and licking the sharp juice off her fingers.

'Inverness and Edinburgh.'

She glanced at him trying to see the Scottish features beneath the tan. Thick tattooed arms in a cut-off rock t-shirt. Barrel chest. Stocky. Hair shaved at the sides and curling dark blonde on top. Laughing eyes. They clinked their glasses together and he poured his drink straight down his throat, washing the glass before she'd taken a second sip. He grinned with his whole face and his mad eyes sparkled. For a moment she thought about adding him to her tattooed men collection. Sensitive Marshall who had 'meet is murder' across his thin, blue-white chest. Too sensitive to tell the tattoo girl that she'd spelled it wrong. She remembered how he'd always managed to sleep with a gap between them, even in the single bed of his student bedsit. She remembered the turquoise nylon sheets which caught on her toenails. He would pull the thin duvet over his head to drown out the sounds of the animal screams from the nearby abattoir and curl up into a ball. Once, when she'd been waiting at the bus stop in the morning in yesterday's clothes and yesterday's mouth, she'd had the feeling she was being watched and looked up, startled to find twenty sheep eyes gazing at her between the slats of a truck.

'I used to think it was the mental hospital across the road,' Marshall had once explained, 'but when that was shut down I realised.' That night, drifting off to sleep beside him, his bony elbows digging into her back, she'd wondered about whether it was wise to go out with someone who cared more about animals than people.

Marshall hadn't been her first tattooed man. That had been bad boy John. He'd had so many tattoos his arm was a blur of faded green and blue and she could never make any of them out distinctly. Fish and stars and crescent moons, odd letters and symbols criss-crossed, reflecting a year, a mood, or a country. On Fridays he would collect her from school and she would pull her long pleated skirt between her legs and clamber onto his bike. She'd close her eyes and lean against his back; cheap leather and cheaper aftershave. As they'd roared away from the school gates she would imagine she was somewhere else. He'd turned out not to be such a bad boy in the end. Sadly.

The cowboy-hatted band in the corner struck up a country version of 'I'm Your Man'. The barman sang along tunelessly as he flipped up glasses and pulled out bottles. Poured drinks with one hand, scooped up ice with the other. He was putting on a show for her. She slid down from the bar stool and went outside to find Jesse.

Pitch black. Even at ten o'clock the humidity hit her as soon as she stepped outside and sweat formed above her upper lip. She pulled her short curls back from her head and gazed beyond the wooden porch to the shapes sitting around the tables. Groups chattered quietly around long wooden benches, fans spinning slowly above them. Everything happened slowly here; except night falling. That was like someone had switched off a light. Not like mid-summer at home where dusk drifted into dawn with no dark in between.

'Eve,' Jesse called, waving her over. As she approached the voice, the dark shapes became a couple that were sitting at a table littered with beer bottles and ashtrays, across from Jesse. He pulled her towards him, wrapping his arm around her waist and crushing her. She still enjoyed feeling small next to him.

'This is my first wife,' he said to his new best friends. The loudness of his voice showing the amount of beers that he'd drunk. Eve smiled like she hadn't heard it before. The couple looked uncomfortable for a moment before the woman leaned over to shake her hand.

'Glad to know you,' she said. 'I'm Mary Beth.'

'I wish my first wife had been as pretty as you,' the man said, clasping her hand in both his warm ones and looking into her eyes as though he'd known her forever and liked her almost as long. 'Then maybe I wouldn't have left her.'

'Carl!' Mary Beth nudged his ribs with her elbows but she was smiling. When Eve looked closer she could see that the woman was more of a girl; anxious green eyes in a thin tanned face, long blonde hair. The sort of pretty that wasn't going to last. Right now, in her short skirt and tight top, she looked like a tired cheerleader. The man was older than her; early forties maybe. Mary Beth held onto his hand as though she would drown if she ever let go and Carl looked back at her like he'd won her in the lottery.

'So what brings y'all to South Carolina?' Mary Beth asked, her voice sugar granules in honey.

'We got married yesterday. On the beach.' It was the easiest explanation. They'd decided to get married on Saturday and done it on Tuesday. Worn flip flops and white t-shirts with bride and groom written on them with thick black markers. After the ceremony, witnessed by two giggling teenagers in bikinis, Jesse had pulled her into the sea where the words on their t-shirts had ran and blurred. They'd dived under the waves and she'd lost the toe ring he'd bought her.

'I hope it's not an omen,' she'd called, before another wave came and salt water filled her mouth.

He'd dived beneath the waves, pulling it up into the air triumphantly and handed it to her. 'A good one?' They'd tried to kiss but a new wave had pulled her away and she'd swum under them and out to meet more.

'Oh wow, guys. You hear that Carl? We're here for our anniversary ourselves,' she confided. 'Eight months.'

'Oh,' Eve said. 'Super.' Super? Had she really said super? The more she lived abroad the more British-off-the-telly she was becoming.

'That calls for a drink,' Carl said, waving to the waiter and indicating beers all round.

A couple of hours and some more drinks later she and Jesse walked along the side of the road together. No pavements in this country for cars. Headlights came towards them and veered away. Eve felt damp with sweat. Jesse's arm was heavy around her shoulder and she shrugged it off. He drifted a little into the road and she grabbed his arm to steady him. A horn blasted. The noise shocking in the dark and her heart beat faster. They passed row after row of similar motels. Their neon lights claiming 'vacancy' or less usually 'no vacancy.' Eve thought that they looked exactly like the motels in *Betty Blue* and *Psycho*. Earlier on Jesse had jumped into the shower behind her wielding a butter knife and she'd fallen to the floor and writhed, pretending to pluck out her eye.

They'd left the air conditioning on in their room and the cool air was welcome, her sweat going cold on her skin. Jesse collapsed onto the king sized bed. Still clothed. Arms and legs splayed out. She poured two glasses of water from the fridge and left one on the table next to his side. She kicked off her denim cut-offs, pulled her damp t-shirt over her head and slung her bra across the room where it hooked around the door handle. She climbed into bed beside Jesse and pulled the sheet up over both of them. She tried to wrap herself round him but he was too large and she was already too hot again. Never mind. In the morning she'd wake up with him wrapped around her and she'd push him off. Two weeks and it had already become a routine. 'Night,' she whispered thinking he wouldn't hear her. But suddenly he was wide awake.

'I'm not just your first husband am I Eve?' he asked.

She slipped her hand inside his t-shirt and ran her fingers lightly across his chest. She could smell his slightly sweaty smell.

'Last, sweetheart,' she said. Instantly, it seemed, he fell asleep.

Her last tattooed man had been Paul. They'd got their tattoos together.

Davy looked at his samples. It wasn't going to work. He tried to care but found that he couldn't. Time for a break. He wandered outside the lab to have a cigarette, switching on his phone as he walked. Along the path the ducklings followed their mother onto the pond. A new set. Again. How many had that been? He really had to get another job. His phone beeped in the pocket of his lab coat and he pulled it out. Eve. Last time he'd heard from her had been a short e-mail from Thailand. She'd met a guy. Another one. 'Not like the usual travelling Americans on their college vacation,' she'd written. 'He doesn't have the ability to pull out an ironed pair of long shorts and a washing power white t-shirt from the depths of a shiny rucksack. No 1950s hairstyle.' This one was different, southern, she'd said. He slowed her down.

Davy tried to imagine a slowed down Eve but his imagination didn't stretch that far.

She was laid-back, Eve, well as laid-back as a woman got. But slow? Nah. 'Does he understand irony?' he'd e-mailed back. Her reply had been instant. Two o'clock in the morning over there. Must have been another one of her insomniac nights. Eve thought sleeping took up too much time. 'You live and then you die,' she'd once said, waving her beer around and slopping it over the sides as they'd walked around Kelvingrove Park at dawn, talking about everything and anything and nothing. 'And while you live you might as well LIVE.' It had made sense at the time. All those late night/early morning conversations had made sense at the time. What had they found to talk about, the seven of them? Had there ever been a lull in the conversation? Except when they'd all been stoned at the same time. When Susy had curled into a ball and fallen asleep on his shoulder, not wanting to go to bed and miss anything and he'd had to remove the lighted cigarette from between her fingers. When Deborah had rolled another joint along an album cover. Wasted and intent. He remembered her trying to teach a joint rolling master class once; Eve and him carefully following her instructions. Paul watching from the sidelines suggesting that someone should write into 'The Generation Game'. His had ended up like a French horn; Eve's had looked OK from the outside but when you took a draw the roach came out and your mouth filled with tobacco. After that they'd left Deborah in charge of joint rolling. 'It's nice to have a role,' she'd said dryly. What had he been thinking, all those late nights?

'Americans do get irony,' her reply had said. 'That's one of the many things I've learned in my travels. They're just well-mannered. They accept what you're saying 'cause the alternative would be rude. It's the Brits who don't understand them. Americans might think you're a prat. They'd just never let you know.'

David stubbed out his cigarette on the ashtray against the wall of the lab block and strolled back to his office. He'd run some calculations based on the new results and then give up for the day.

Would he prefer to know if people thought he was a prat? Once he wouldn't have cared. He'd just think they hadn't got the joke. Their loss. Now? He wasn't sure.

He thought about Eve's text. 'I got married today,' it had said.

He wondered who would tell Paul.

The Guddle

Vicky MacKenzie

Rock pools disappointed me as a child because they never looked like the illustrations in my *Ladybird Book of the Seashore*. These always showed a starfish and a hermit crab at the bottom of the pool, with maroon anemones artfully arranged around the sides. In reality rock pools always looked empty, just a clear pocket of water with a few strips of seaweed, and a couple of limpets that I never managed to prise from their rocky home. Now I'm older I'm more patient. I see transparent shrimps scuffing up the sand and occasionally spot a tiny green crab scurrying out from under a pebble. Patience still isn't my strong point, mind.

'Marilyn!' My friends are calling me. I've been staring into the rock pools while they mess around in the surf, boys picking up girls and threatening to chuck them in the water. Not my idea of fun, the water's bloody freezing.

'Marilyn!' Kath is waving manically. 'We're going for fish and chips!'

It's not a name you hear on a young person anymore. My mother named me after Marilyn Monroe, if you can believe anything so daft. She thought Marilyn was the most beautiful woman ever to walk God's earth, and that if she named me after her, I would be beautiful too. It didn't work: my eyes are too close together and my lips are thin. A lipstick lasts me forever, I've nothing to smear it on.

'Coming!' I give her a wave and brace myself for the noise and energy of my friends. Kath is 25 going on 15. Ian's her boyfriend, they've been together for ten years: everyone expects they'll get married. Good for them I say, but I can't imagine being with anyone for so long. Barry's my cousin and he's 30. It's his car we use when we go out, like today's outing to Brighton. Then there's Bess – she's 27 and moons around Barry till everyone gets embarrassed for her. She can't get into her head that he doesn't fancy her. Poor girl. One day she'll meet her prince and all that. I'm the baby at 22; everyone says I'm the quiet one.

Today's trip is meant to be about cheering me up – my boyfriend Mark and I split up, and then I got made redundant from my job in the card shop. I don't really mind about the job, I didn't think I'd be there for life, but I don't know what to do with myself now. I feel sort of loose and reckless, like I've been unpinned and could fly away with the slightest breath of wind. I'm like a speck of dust, blowing over the surface of things.

We crunch up the pebbles to the promenade and cross the road to the chippie. There are bikers revving at the lights and one of them gives me a cheeky wave. I think about running over and jumping on the back of his bike, zooming off to some other life, but I just smile.

The chippie's steamed up and busy. We stand around discussing what to have. I want cod and chips, easy. I like chippies, there's something so familiar about them: the greasy smell, the funny wooden forks, the jars of pickled eggs. It's funny how they display the eggs on the counter – as if you might be tempted. I did eat one once, for a laugh. We went clubbing afterwards and I felt like I had a whole boiled egg stuck half way down my gullet for the rest of the night.

There seems to be some kind of argument up at the counter: a tall thin boy with a shaved head is arguing with the woman serving him. He's got cheekbones like razorblades and his t-shirt's tight as a scab. The raised voices stop and he points a finger in the woman's face before spinning round and walking out. As he passes me he catches my eye but keeps walking.

We get our food and head back to the beach to eat. It's getting dark now and there are groups of young people sitting around smoky fires and barbecues with cans of beer. From the pier the distant thump of music drifts over and the warm air carries the smell of candyfloss and fried doughnuts. This is good place to be, I think. I'm glad I came out today.

I suddenly become aware that the boy from the chippie is walking alongside me. I turn to sneak a look at him but he's looking right at me and he winks.

'I thought ah might be seeing youse again,' he says.

'Oh?' It comes out snootier than I mean it to.

'Aye. Ah were right an' all.'

'I guess you were.' I smile this time. I like how he looks, all skinny and sure of himself.

'What's yer name, anyway?'

'Marilyn.' I pull a face as I say it.

'Suits yer.' He reaches over and tugs a strand of my short black hair.

He leans in to me and whispers, 'You can call me Kyle.' His breath smells of vodka.

The others have walked on ahead but Kath turns and gives me a little thumbs up. I roll my eyes at her, but then smile. Being chatted up is probably just what I need.

'I'm going to eat over here,' I say to Kyle, pointing at the rock pools. 'Do you want to come?'

We perch on a flattish rock, still warm from the sun, and I open up the newspaper wrapped around my fish and chips.

'I've been looking into these pools all day,' I tell him. 'Haven't seen a thing.'

'Where ah'm from we call that guddling,' he says. 'Looking intae rock pools. Shame we dinnae have a net.'

'I'm a bit old for shrimping,' I say, but it comes out all sneery.

'Och, you're only a young thing!' He sounds like an old man giving advice although he hardly looks twenty. He squeezes my knee, bare below my denim shorts.

'My mum told me to watch out for boys like you.'

'Alright, convent girl.' He puts his hand higher, where my skin's paler and I don't bother taking the razor. I put my fish and chips on the rock and stand up.

'It means other stuff too, guddling does,' he says. He stands up too and turns me round so my back's to him. Then he puts his arms round me; it feels good, sort of comforting. Then he puts his hands on my breasts, ever so gently. 'When you tickle a trout from the river bed.

That's called guddling.'

I brush his hands away and poke a flip-flopped toe into the water. 'When he was a boy my great uncle Jack went to Scarborough and plucked a six foot eel from a rock pool,' I blurt.

'Aye, did he now?'

'Yep.'

'Sounds like quite a man, your uncle Jack.'

'He's dead now. He was a greengrocer and he had a girl up against a sack of potatoes once. Had to brush the soil off her thighs before she could put her stockings back on, and Betty, his wife, was out front serving all the time he was doing it. That was his story anyway. I liked my Aunt Betty. She's dead now too, eaten by cancer when I was still a kid.'

I don't know why I'm telling him all this. It's as if by talking I can put off whatever else is to come, can put off the future. I think about what else I can say. I see he doesn't have any food himself. 'What was all that argey-bargey about, back there in the chippie?'

'Ach, the daft bint wouldnae take my money.'

'What's wrong with it? Make it yourself?'

'It's Scottish, that's all tha's wrong with it. She refused to take it, acted like she'd never seen it before in her life.'

'Is it different, then? Can I see?'

'Are youse gonnae rob me?'

'Yup.'

He laughs. 'I'd like to see you try.' He hands me a tenner from his wallet. It's got Walter Scott one side and a picture of a huge stone bridge on the other side. *Glenfinnan Viaduct* is written at the top. 'It's pretty,' I say.

Suddenly he grabs my wrist and looks into my eyes. 'Where do you want to die?'

'Well, not here. I don't think I'm ready.' I laugh but it comes out like a yelp. He lets go and stares at the sea.

'Me, I wanna die in Scotland. I wanna be like one of them shepherds out on the hills all his life, and when it's my time I'm just gonnae lay down and die. The ravens can have me until ma bones are white.'

'Ravens!' I scoff, 'You don't get ravens in this country.'

He smiles at me, like I'm a total know-nothing. 'You might not get them here, in these overcrowded parts,' he gestures at the built-up promenade, the hotels and cinemas. 'But you get them in the hills in Scotland alright. Clever creatures an' all. Summat in their eyes, you know they've always got the measure of you.'

He looks at me, like he's trying to tell me he's a raven too, that he has the measure of me.

'Tell yer what,' he says. 'How about I write my number on this tenner, and then I give it to yer. You'll owe me, then.'

'I don't want to owe you,' I say. 'Why don't you just text it to me or write it on a bit of paper?'

'Cos I reckon if yer think yer owe me, you'll ring me.'

'Got a pen?' I ask.

'No, but I bet you have.'

I open my handbag and take out a pen. He does have the measure of me: I always have pens, a notebook, tissues, an emergency bar of chocolate and a book of stamps. I'm like a sodding Girl Guide.

He writes on the tenner and then slips it in the back pocket of my shorts.

'Ah've gotta go now, but it was nice meetin' yer, Marilyn.' He kisses me hard on the lips and slips his tongue in, just for a second. Then he's gone.

I sit down on the pebbles and eat what's left of my fish and chips. Then I unfold the tenner and look for Kyle's number, but he hasn't put it. Instead he's written *Be kind to yourself.* I slip it back in my pocket. The tide's gone further out and there are more rock pools exposed, the rising moon reflected in each one like silver coins scattered across the water. It's completely dark now and the pools are black and shiny; they aren't going to reveal their secrets tonight.

Inside Outside

Ruth Thomas

Brown Owl, a.k.a Sandra Waites, turned up at Catherine's house at five thirty. She was dressed as a witch and carrying a pumpkin on a length of green raffia, its glowing face cut out lop-sided and peculiar.

Catherine felt quite shocked. For some reason she'd imagined that Brown Owl would turn up as Brown Owl.

'Wow!' said Catherine's mother, opening the door and casting a pale golden light from the hallway across the path, 'you look...'

But she trailed off. She didn't seem to know what Sandra Waites looked like.

'Ready for the witching hour, Catherine?' Sandra Waites asked, in her upbeat way.

Catherine peered at her. She recognised the witch costume: she'd seen it on sale at Sainsbury's the day before. It was made of some slippery sort of black material. There was a pair of striped black and purple tights to go with it, and a stiff, starchy-looking hat, and a wand that lit up if you pressed a button. Sandra Waites had also invested in a pair of pointy shoes with buckles. They were like a picture Catherine had seen once, of Oliver Cromwell's shoes.

'I know I'm here a bit early,' she said to Catherine's mother, 'but I've got to scoop up Miss Carvell and half the Brownies in the neighbourhood before we can even get started!'

'Really?' Catherine's mother replied. She sounded slightly alarmed. And standing in front of her, Catherine suddenly felt her mother's hands, gentle on her shoulders, and she wanted to turn round and hide her face in her apron. Her mother had been making a pie – she'd been standing in the kitchen making pastry for an apple pie – and Catherine wanted to stay with her for the rest of the night. *I don't want to go guising with Mrs Waites*! she wanted to burst out. But she was seven now, and too old for that kind of performance.

Sandra Waites was saying something else now. She had adopted the tone adults used sometimes – a low, serious kind of drone that Catherine found dull and intriguing at the same time.

'Have you heard anything from Mary? How's Mary doing?' she was murmuring.

And Catherine's mother didn't reply for a moment. Then she said:

'No, I haven't seen her at all, Sandra. I honestly can't imagine how she's doing.'

'No,' Sandra Waites said, frowning. All three of them stared down for a moment at her terrible pointy witch shoes, positioned there on their doorstep. 'It's absolutely awful,' she added.

'Yes,' said Catherine's mother. 'It's just too awful for words.'

Sandra Waites sighed heavily.

'I didn't really know what to *do* about tonight,' she said. 'I'd thought maybe I should cancel. But then I thought, you know: *life goes on*. It's one of those lessons the girls have to learn.'

'Hmm,' said Catherine's mother.

Catherine looked up again and out, past the form of Sandra Waites, and down their garden path. She could see the pumpkin she and her mother had carved earlier that day and placed at their gate, lit from inside with her father's bike light. And she thought: *They're talking about Billy*. They were talking about a small boy, the little brother of her friend and fellow Brownie, Eve Wiseman. Billy was two years old – had been two years old – but he had died two days earlier. He'd had something called a Hole in the Heart. Three days ago he'd been alive, and now he wasn't. Her mother had told her when she'd got back from school on Tuesday. They'd been sitting at the kitchen table eating digestive biscuits and drinking tea, and she had said:

'Cathy, sweetheart, I'm so sorry to tell you this, but Billy Wiseman died today.'

And for a moment she'd wondered who Billy Wiseman was. And then she'd realised. And something about the digestive biscuit had gone wrong in Catherine's mouth. It had suddenly felt too dry and too big for her to swallow, and so she'd taken it back out of her mouth and put it on her plate.

'Why?' she said.

'He had a hole in his heart,' said her mother.

'A hole in his heart?' Catherine repeated, a picture of Billy Wiseman floating into her head. Billy Wiseman with a wrongly-made heart. It was hard to comprehend that he was not alive. It felt much more likely that he would still be sitting in the Wisemans' living room, yelling and banging a plastic xylophone with a stick.

'But how did he ever *live* with a hole in his heart?' she asked.

And she tried not to imagine what that might look like.

'It's just what they call it,' her mother had replied, her eyes suddenly brimming with tears. 'It's not like... I don't really know... what it means. It just means his heart doesn't... didn't... work properly. He was born with it like that. But no-one thought he was going to die...' she said, and then she started to sob. And Catherine had sat for a moment, with the digestive biscuit on the plate in front of her. Then she had stood up, walked around the table and stroked her mother's cheek. And then she had left the room.

'So,' Sandra Waites was saying, her voice its normal volume again and directed straight at Catherine. 'I *do* like your costume, Missy. Very swish. Are you Dracula?'

'No, I'm Morticia,' said Catherine.

'Well! Very fancy!'

Nothing ever, ever surprised Sandra Waites, about anything.

'And I hope you've got some weird and wonderful jokes worked out tonight, then, for the trick or treating?'

'Yes,' said Catherine.

'Tell us, then.'

Catherine stiffened and tried to remember. Last Halloween she and Eve Wiseman had sung a song they'd made up. They'd sung 'At Halloween time the witches fly on their broomsticks into the sky...'

They'd both dressed up as witches too, only they hadn't gone out guising with the Brownies because they weren't old enough. They'd still only been Rainbows. So they'd just gone guising on their own, with Mr Wiseman following a few paces behind them, to the doors along Eve's street. Eve had had a small besom broom from British Home Stores and had put on some glittery eye shadow. Catherine had worn a dress made from a kind of grey gossamer, which her mother had found in Remnant Kings.

'...bubb-ling stews and witches' brews,' they'd warbled into the darkness, 'I wouldn't go out if I were you...'

And they'd earned a whole stash of Crunchie bars and Bounties and Parma Violets and Drumsticks and little chocolates shaped like eyeballs and pumpkins. And when they'd gone back to Eve's house, Billy had been sitting in a high chair, eating rice pudding.

Eve wasn't going to be with them this year, of course. Nobody knew where the Wisemans were, at all.

'So, Miss Morticia,' Sandra Waites said to Catherine. 'What's your joke, then? What are you going to be saying,' she added with a bright, stiff smile, 'when we knock at people's doors?'

Catherine breathed in slowly, and breathed out again.

'What is the scariest side of a haunted house?' she asked.

Sandra Waites blinked. Her eyelids, Catherine noticed, were painted purple. She looked as if she'd been in a fight.

'Say that again, sweetheart. A bit more slowly.'

Catherine cleared her throat.

'What,' she asked, 'is the scariest side of a haunted house?'

Sandra Waites looked up at Catherine's mother, a different kind of smile on her face now; one of those miserable, upside-down smiles that adults sometimes had.

'The scariest side of a haunted house?' she repeated. 'Well, I really don't know, darling.'

Catherine waited. She knew about comic timing. She said:

'The inside.'

Silence fell.

'I don't get it,' Sandra Waites said.

'Ha! Neither did I at first,' Catherine's mother exclaimed, still holding onto Catherine's shoulders. 'It's quite subtle, Sandra. It's one of those jokes you have to think about.'

Sandra Waites frowned. Her hat had slipped forwards a little: it looked like it might not last the night.

'It's because,' Catherine explained – she felt she would have to explain – 'it's scarier *inside* a haunted house than *outside*.'

'Oh,' said Sandra Waites. 'Yes, I see. Right. Well.'

She didn't laugh.

'Well,' she said, 'that certainly *is* weird and wonderful, Catherine. Anyway, we can't hang around chatting all evening, can we! We've got neighbours to spook!'

And, leaning forward suddenly, she grabbed Catherine's hand and dragged her out onto the path. She was like the Wicked Witch of the West. She was like the witches Roald Dahl wrote about.

'I'll have her back by seven,' she stated.

'Have fun, darling,' Catherine's mother said unsurely, and then she closed the door, and Catherine and Sandra Waites were on their own.

The previous week, before anyone had known Billy Wiseman would die, they'd had a craft session at Brownies. They'd all had to make little witches out of pipe cleaners and black paper – Halloween being a long-drawn-out thing with Sandra Waites – then they had sellotaped their witches onto small twigs they'd pulled off the chestnut tree outside the church hall (the twigs were meant to be broomsticks) and put them on display on the hall's reception table. Catherine had been proud of her witch. She had liked the shape of her little face and the blue of her eyes and the way she sat so well on her broomstick. She enjoyed the craft evenings at Brownies, mainly because Sandra Waites didn't intervene. Craft wasn't her kind of thing, and so she always let another woman, a young trainee teacher called Miss Carvell, help out instead. Miss Carvell was second-in-command. Miss Carvell had soft, plump, white hands and smelled of Cold Cream soap.

'That's a really lovely witch,' she'd said to Catherine. 'Has she got a name?'

Which nobody else had asked her.

'We need to get a move on,' Sandra Waites announced, striding along the pavement.

They had three other girls to pick up – Eleanor, Tamsin and Macy. Then they had to go round for Miss Carvell at Leamington Terrace. Then they had to pick up five more Brownies, before they could begin guising. And only after that could they head off to the church hall for the party.

'Come on,' said Sandra Waites.

And the evening spread out before Catherine, loud and dark and without any sense of an ending. She'd also forgotten her joke, she realised, now she was standing outside in the blackness. It had just gone clean out of her head. All she could remember was one Eve Wiseman had been going to say, about bats.

'It's going to be a smashing night,' Sandra Waites proclaimed as they continued up the pavement in their cold, slippery costumes. There was going to be Wink Murder, she added, and there were going to be doughnuts suspended from a washing line, and a pumpkin competition, and that game where you had to cut up a chocolate bar with a plastic knife, while wearing a pair of gloves –

'What's it called, that game?'

'I don't know,' Catherine said. She had always hated that game. And looking down at her party shoes, the tips of them, peeping out from her black dress hem, she felt suddenly very tired. She felt very tired and old. She felt as old as the world. The last two days seemed to have gone on for such a long time; they had just been so odd and timeless, at school and at home, since Billy Wiseman had died.

'I think maybe it's called the Chocolate Bar game,' she said.

'Really?' Sandra Waites replied, unconvinced. 'Well, I think we should give it a more Halloweeny name, don't you, darling? Like *Operation* or something.'

And they crossed the road and rounded the corner of the street.

And they were, Catherine realised, walking straight down the Wiseman's street.

They were walking right past their house. Number 32 Leamington Place.

'Oh, Mrs Waites –' she began, feeling suddenly very ashamed.

Because the Wiseman's house was just so completely dark and empty and private and she knew they really shouldn't be blundering past it. It was too sad a house for them to be walking past like that. It was too bare. She hadn't seen Eve Wiseman for ages, not since Art Club the previous Tuesday. They had all gone away, and nobody knew where; they had just gone away. There was no car in the driveway and no lights on in the windows, and the garden looked so empty it almost seemed not to be there at all. Normally, when she and her mother walked past, they would see the Wisemans sitting in their yellow living room with their dog, watching television. Or they might see the light on in Eve's little upstairs room. Or in the summer time, sometimes, the whole family would be outside, in the garden. She looked up at the moon above the Wiseman's roof – the huge, white, sad moon and wondered what might have happened to Billy Wiseman's soul. Where did souls go? Did they go anywhere? Did they stay the same age? Did they get looked after? And she felt a great kind of hollowness in her chest.

'Anyway, trust me, it's going to be one of the best Halloween parties ever!' Sandra Waites continued as they ploughed past in their costumes, towards Miss Carvell's house.

Miss Carvell's doorbell was one of those ding-dong ones. You put your finger on it and it made a high, ringing note, and then you took your finger off and it made a different note, about four pitches lower.

Ding.

Dong.

'Merry,' Sandra Waites observed, taking off her witch's hat before bending to adjust her tights. They'd spiralled around her legs slightly.

There was no pumpkin on Miss Carvell's path, Catherine noticed, or perched beside her front door with a tealight in it. There were no ghost-shaped fairy lights or ghouls or incident tape or skeletons or dangling spiders. The whole of her front garden looked as if it had nothing whatsoever to do with Halloween.

'I thought Susan was putting a pumpkin out,' Sandra Waites said, as a light went on in the hallway and they heard Miss Carvell approaching the door. 'I thought you were putting a pumpkin out, Susan,' she continued to Miss Carvell as she opened the door.

Miss Carvell stood in the doorway. She was dressed all in white. But she was not a ghost: Catherine could see that straight away. She was just wearing a white sweatshirt and some off-white jeans. The sweatshirt had a scattering of diamante sequins in the shape of a bird. Also, she was wearing a pair of white calf-length boots with tassles. Catherine could smell her Cold Cream soap smell, too. It seemed to scent the whole house.

'What are *you* going as?' Sandra Waites asked, her eyes round and fringed with purple. 'A cowgirl?'

'I'm not going,' said Miss Carvell.

Sandra Waites stared.

'*What*?' she demanded.

'I'm not going,' Miss Carvell said again. 'Didn't you get my phone message?'

'Your *phone message*?' Sandra Waites repeated. 'When did you leave it?'

'About two hours ago.'

Sandra Waites was momentarily speechless. She stood very still, and a sudden cold breeze flicked at the hem of her witch's dress. She said:

'Well, I wouldn't have picked up any phone message *two hours ago,* Susan, because *two hours ago* I was standing in *Tesco's,* buying *party food!*'

And a vision came into Catherine's head when she said this, of Tesco's Halloween aisle, with all its luminous skeleton suits and foam devil's horns and plastic pumpkins. Of Sandra Waites, a.k.a Brown Owl, grabbing snake sweets and plastic fangs and fake cobwebs, and putting them in her trolley.

'So is anything wrong?' Sandra Waites snapped at Miss Carvell. 'Are you not feeling well or something, Susan? I mean, I'm not being funny but I *am* concerned about the adult-child ratio now! That's all I'm saying. You know, maybe we're going to have to...'

'I just didn't feel like celebrating,' Miss Carvell interrupted. 'That's all.'

And she smiled down at Catherine.

'I just didn't think it was the right thing to be doing,' she said.

Sandra Waites did not reply. She simply stood there on Miss Carvell's path in her witch costume and pointy shoes. She looked, it occurred to Catherine, a bit like the Wicked Witch of the West, just after Dorothy had thrown the bucket of water over her.

'But life goes on, Susan!' she croaked after a moment. 'Doesn't it? It's a lesson the girls have to learn. You know: we have to deal with reality.'

'I know,' said Miss Carvell. 'But is this reality? Or is it just dressing up in fake witches' outfits?'

Mrs Waites looked at Miss Carvell and Miss Carvell looked at Mrs Waites. Then Mrs Waites put her hat on her head and took a step backwards.

'Fine, Susan!' she said. 'That's *absolutely fine*! No doubt I'll be breaking all the regulations now. No doubt all the parents will fall on me like a ton of bricks when they find out about the adult-child ratio tonight, but that's not a problem! Off we go then, Catherine,' she commanded, projecting her hand out for Catherine to hold.

And Catherine made a decision. It felt like the first decision she'd ever made. She said: 'No thanks, Mrs Waites: I'd rather stay with Miss Carvell.'

On their way back home, they walked past the Wiseman's house. And when Catherine looked up she saw that a light was on, at the very top of the house. It was Eve's light. A little rectangle of yellow. And something, some prickle of sorrow made her shudder. She tried to recall the last time she'd seen Billy Wiseman, and wished she'd said something nice to him. She wished she'd played with him for a while, at least. Building bricks or something, or a puzzle, or Peekaboo. She wished she'd known.

'Eve's back,' Miss Carvell said. 'I bet she'd love to see you soon, Catherine.'

'Yes.'

And something odd seemed to be happening to the shape of her mouth, and the way her voice was coming out of it. It was all low and thick, the way her mother's had been, that teatime.

'Last Halloween,' she said, 'me and Eve made up a song about witches.'

'Did you, love?'

And they walked the rest of the way in silence, Catherine in black and Miss Carvell in white, past all the candle-lights, down all the dark streets.

The Undulations of Mr Whisper

Frances Corr

Mr Whisper stood at the draining board. His mouth was a line although at one side it wanted to go up because he couldn't help but find life endlessly amusing. Here he was concerned with arranging tumblers in such a way that they would be spared destruction by the laws of gravity, should the washing machine below shake them loose.

Looking down he caught sight of his feet and was grateful. Two broad feet with five toes each. An open fan of metatarsi that felt no shyness with the earth. However, he knew that care must be taken to avoid a meeting of glass and naked foot.

Drying foam off his hands with a chequered cloth his head turned in the direction of where he might like to go next. The foam called his attention back to the webs of his fingers, and he marvelled at the bubbles before their transition into cloth dampness. Then hung the tea towel through the handle of the oven.

Now where was I going, he said to himself and with that the line of his mouth rose up again at one side. This journey ahead he was anticipating, this operation to be put into action, to travel an estimated eight steps to the chair that would kindly accommodate his weight, leaving the feet free of their purpose for a little while.

He wiggled his toes and realised he was in the chair without the journey. He enjoyed the way his weight sank and the joys of a supported back, but had no recollection of getting there, whether the eight steps were a close estimation or wildly inaccurate, and worried for a moment that he may have missed some action.

The back of his hair was all curls. They rode over the collar of his shirt. It was an easy man's shirt, the collar with no formality. Cardigan buttons led the way down to his hands which were clasped in a loose basket, settled on his tummy, slightly off-centre.

Then a leaf caught his eye out the window. It was a leaf that while still attached, was going its own way. The rest of the tree seemed stationary, but this singular leaf was boisterous, twisting, turning and flapping like a wild thing, as if it occupied a space where the weather was different. Mr Whisper was delighted.

He was then faced with a difficult dilemma in his chair. He wanted to put his feet up on the window ledge in front of him but when he did, he could no longer see the leaf. If he positioned the feet to the left a little there was an awkward pull on his hip. If he left them where they were he could twist his body and glimpse the leaf from time to time. He rested back again and enjoyed the feeling so much that he succumbed to the loss of the leaf, satisfying himself with the viewing of it in a freshly made memory.

I'd like a cup of tea, he said to himself. Where is my tea? Initially Mr Whisper was irked. Bothered that his tea wasn't already there beside him, on a handy reachable surface with the handle towards him and steam twirling out of an easy ellipse, he damned himself for not preparing the tea before he sat down.

He glanced round at the kettle, then the floor. This is my chance to see just how many steps there are, he said to himself, and bent forward, rising to his feet. Outside the leaf continued its dramatic display. One leaf alone at sea in hurricane conditions, while the rest sat perfectly still on the calmest of days.

Mr Whisper put his hand on the back of the chair. He didn't enjoy counting his steps. It was as if someone was making him do it. It was boring and he just wanted to get there. As he filled the kettle his mind was still upset and he grumped and wasn't pleased with himself. He couldn't see the leaf, just his little living space and it looked tiny and dull and where was that place he had been? Where had it gone?

He chose a lemon yellow cup. His eye fell on a corner of the drainer where some dirt had taken up residence. It was an awkward corner to clean, the cutlery compartment, so the dirt in its opportunistic manner had commandeered the area. The lemon yellow cup offered some balm to the rippling mind of Mr Whisper. Its brightness outshone the dirty corner as he held it in his hand like a blinding sun.

The tea is in the cup and I can't remember making it, realised Mr Whisper. Puzzled he ran through his very recent past. But no, there was no memory of tea bag, cupboard nor hot water pouring. Ah well, said Mr Whisper, his mouth going up again at one side. I have it now, and he carried the cup of tea in one hand back to his chair.

The cup warmed and comforted his holding palms as rain lashed down outside and everything grew dark. He felt lucky and cosy. So many raindrops forming lines through the air all at the same angle. The lines reminded him of lino he knew as a boy, patterned with rods of different colours. It had fascinated him. Where would that lino be now, he wondered. Back in the earth, not too deeply but somewhere relatively near the surface. The leaves outside nodded as the rain knocked every single one. He could no longer see the wayward individual.

Mr Whisper liked the sound of the rain. It was comforting the way the collective sound of the raindrops stotted off the ground and everything in its path. It settled the mind. It made more sound than the nonsense in his head. Nonsense that went back and forth and roundabout discussing itself in tiring spirals to no avail. And the rain continued down as he fell into pleasant slumber.

Some time later Mr Whisper's eyelids were filled with sunlight and he opened them. Birds were chattering as his eyes fell on his hands. They were huge and at peace on his lap. Incredible to think they were once the hands of a baby. He couldn't remember it but a hand had fascinated him then just as much as it did now, turning it this way and that on front of his face, lost in awe at this wonder. His eyes glided over the small table where the grain of the wood was cast in pleasing ovals. A long shadow stretched from his teacup. He hadn't even drunk his tea. Mr Whisper realised this and laughed out loud. The air filled with more birdsong and intermittent traffic noises. The washing machine was silent, having finished its cycle. There wasn't anywhere else in the world where Mr Whisper would rather be just now, so deep was his peace.

And the air billowed in and out of his nostrils as if someone else was doing it for him and he loved being alive. His feet felt great. He wouldn't have believed they could feel much greater had he not placed them up on the window ledge and felt the wonder vibrate up his legs. The wellbeing evoked a memory, an image of his back when it was young and fit, more muscled in the days when he broke a sweat every day. The memory brought no pain with it. Curious, thought Mr Whisper. He loved the memory and he loved the strong back but there was no sense of loss. Where is it? he thought. Is it under my chair, is it behind the curtain. Will it arrive in the post. And the line of his mouth curled up uncontrollably at one end.

Half the sky was blue and half was exciting grey. He took a notion in his mind to run about the grass in tight circles. A thought disturbed Mr Whisper. I'm wasting my time, was the thought. He was gutted at this news. My neat expectations of myself have not worked out. And a list of occupations developed at speed in his head – empty the washing machine, go to the shop...

Then he decided that this was actually a very good use of his time and a sigh of relief followed. He noticed he had taken his feet down from the window ledge in readiness. There was no action from the leaf.

Mr Whisper wanted a banana. For a moment he noticed how fast he was moving. The banana was gone in less than two minutes. He had been looking forward to it for much longer than that. He had used it as a milestone in his day, to get him through in case the time should drag and needed broken up. Now he was left looking at the skin. It had not been everything he'd built it up to be. He wished he could rewind and eat the banana again. Noticing it this time so he could at least feel like he had eaten it.

Mr Whisper had another thought. It pierced the future. I'll never get it done, were the words trying to come together from a scatter in him. They tried to fit together to form a fear, but there was a space in the middle that prevented it. Leaving the words powerless and disintegrating. Yellow featured somewhere. Floral yellow.

Mr Whisper recalled a particular pair of trousers. He had called them his depressing trousers. The crotch had hung too low and prevented him from getting a good stride in. They would be a good reason for not going to the shop. As it turned out he had overcome the waste debate in his head and settled for putting them out. They can go back to the earth via the landfill site, he had concluded. The thought of now being in comfortable trousers excited him greatly. As did buying salad leaves to nourish himself with at this fine expansive time of year.

As soon as he moved geographically there was a myriad of thought. He found himself in his jacket. The door handle was pushed down and it was his hand that was doing it. Outside there was no rain but Mr Whisper was already braced. Curiously, the inside of Mr Whisper was the same outside as it was when indoors and this gave him an unexpected warmth. He dropped his shoulders and it came with him, the warmth. There was no shock, no shiver. His eyes looked for the trees and his head followed. Then something happened. I don't like the pavements, he thought and his shoulders curled and his pace quickened and windows sped by and it was like he was flying over things, as if someone was pushing him, so that his feet barely touched the ground and he didn't like it and he didn't like the buses going through puddles and the noise of the traffic and the people in the cars and he hated himself and he stopped breathing and his eyes bulged and he went 'fuck'.

Mr Whisper had missed the shop. He'd gone quite a distance past it. Several doorways and windows past it in fact and was forced to do a u-turn, slightly sheepish lest another person might see him. He didn't fear for a dog or a cat seeing him because they wouldn't judge or tell or snigger. Nor the birds for they could already see full well the bizarre movements of the human and cared little as they had the air.

He heard the shop doorbell and stood for a while, gazing at shelves. He waited patiently for the words to arrive in his head. The names of the items he was to purchase.

Someone asked if he needed some help. He had an expression on his face that he hadn't intended, dictated by a rogue thought that made him look unfriendly. It's fine thanks, he answered quickly just to give him the space to catch up with himself.

I can't remember for the life of me what I came here for, thought Mr Whisper, and stood there a while longer bamboozled as a discussion ensued in his head over whether he should have accepted help or not. What could they have done, he thought, if I can't remember what I'm looking for in the first place. I might've just made something up for the sake of saying something. And then went on to worry that he may have been rude. Meanwhile the problem of what he was to buy carried on underneath, and he stood in the shop and saw greyness and felt his past around him when suddenly there it was on front of his eyes illuminated – a can of butter beans. Something is on my side said Mr Whisper and lifted the can as the names of the other items came streaming into his head and he picked up a basket and continued around the shop with a renewed confidence.

On leaving the shop with his messages he looked forward to being back in his chair. His mind, however, thinking it was back in his chair, looked forward to moving around a bit. For a moment Mr Whisper didn't really know where he was, if indeed he was anywhere. The noise of the traffic bothered him. He wanted to punch it in the nose. His hand was braced with try, aching, and he realised this was unnecessary given the fairly easy weight of his carrier bag.

Back in the house it was evening. Mr Whisper took off his jacket. He was tired and hungry and other things simultaneously. It was dressing up time for Mr Whisper's mind. A cacophony of voices and forms. He wanted them all to go away. The words in his head had a rhythm, a sort of hammering on the railway lines. The repetition seemed to hold a sort of attempt at completion, a subtle nailing to the ground. Then he spotted the lemon cup sitting squint, to the right, on a wooden stool with a central dip. He would have a cup of tea. And sit and read a book. Dropping in a round tea bag there was an expression of mirth, a little pursed mouth as if holding it in, and a tell-tale corner of the eye.

Mr Whisper's feet took him and his tea steadily over to the chair. There was no need to count. He sat down and reached for his book. The leaf outside was invisible now amongst the others. He felt good. He opened his book and read a sentence but the reading voice in his head faded towards the end of it. His mind felt heavy and tired at the front. He lifted his tea and spilt it all over the page.

Aw for fucksake, thought Mr Whisper. He watched the letters blow up into balloon words and float out the window. They were yellow. Aw-for-fucksake they read in the air but in fun shaped form, losing all viciousness and with an element of play. As if he should skip after them, whooping.

In this reality however, he would have a badly broken leg as there was quite a drop, and perhaps even a head injury. Mr Whisper smiled and put down his tea and his book. The liquid had already begun to seep into the page but if he was swift enough he could mop the tan puddle that was left in the middle. He reached in his pocket for his man's handkerchief with the central dull blue square in the middle and straight lines around the border and wiped, separating pages to catch the tea on its journey through the book. Then laid it down, open, on the little table where any passing sunlight might catch it and dry it with its warmth. He lifted the lemon cup and wiped its sides and its bottom and the spreading circle underneath and placed it back down, a quarter cup settling.

Mr Whisper opened his handkerchief to view the rest of his tea. Up came his past again and made him down. It made him stop as if there was a cliff edge, then –

a tender wind of attention.

You're ok you are Mr Whisper. You're ok.

And his body breathed up and down and up and down like gently rolling hills.

House of Wax

Tim Turnbull

Even in motion, even as it happened,
even with the sweat of exertion filming
his torso, he knew – *click* – this stays,
a still in his memory; the flutter
of his raincoat stopped dead in mid-
billow; Tall Paul a hundred yards ahead,
kitchen knife brandished, frozen in the street;
car windows ice-glazed, the street frosted,
February, silent. And later, flicking through
the boxes of bagged cards, memorabilia
filed provisionally with board dividers
by genre, director, title, retrieve this
single faded frame and build back
the colour, action, sound, the warmth
of human intimacy, of conflict, of love.

Scarecrow

Tim Turnbull

They have brought him indoors again, Scarecrow,
propped him in the armchair, poured him a nip
of Laphroaig (doubles for themselves) and toast
and laud him, fine splendid fellow that he is:

for did he not bring them glories unbekent
in their lifetimes, class and outright victory
at Scarecrow Festival; did not the beer tent
glow all night, song swell through the district

over misted fields and greening woodland.
Hail to thee, O Flay-crake! O Hodmedod!
O Bogle! they cry, glasses in raised hands,
in honour of their straw-stuffed half-a-god,

and Scarecrow tilts his head as if perplexed:
their panegyric's tinctured with derision,
and rough-handling, not kindness or respect,
distinguishes their weekly depositions.

Tonight a boot was left among the furrows;
tomorrow they'll drag him out and nail him
back up again, nursing filthy hangovers,
and leave him to the mercy of the wind.

Flacking Crombled wi Shommers o Drod an Fistering Sleugh

Hugh McMillan

*In the language of this remote area there are many terms for the feeling you get when you see
a grey mist creeping down a cold hill where some wet sheep are waiting stoically*

Drod (n) Dull indefinable feeling of being involved in a scene that prefigures one's own
death, as in 'This morning my father woke to a peculiar sense of drod'
Sleugh (n) Psychosomatic, but terrifyingly real, sense of nausea, often experienced in
natural surroundings
Drod an sleugh
Fister (verb) To creep sickeningly slowly like an injured beast, or a disease, as in 'Uncle
Ansel is fistering down the road'
Fistering drod
Fistering drod an sleugh
Shommers (n) plural (colloquial) A group of things that might be imagined but are very
real to the person that experiences them
Shommers o drod
Shommers o drod an fistering sleugh
Dwank (adj) (archaic) Black, sodden, wet, often in relation to a carcass, as in 'Last night
I found a dwank horse's head under the duvet'.
Dwank shommers o drod
Dwank an fistering shommers o drod
Dwank shommers o fistering drod
Crombled (adj) Crippled, hunched, incapacitated as if by great age or boredom
Crombled wi drod
Flacking (adj) Too weak to move while simultaneously exasperated
Flacking crombled
Flacking crombled wi drod
Flacking crombled wi shommers o drod an fistering sleugh

Book Launch, Oxford 2009

Hugh McMillan

Tasha is just out of poets' school,
where she was Head Girl,
and Bridget and Dan have the same hat.
They say I'm authentic
but I'm merely filthy drunk
and hanging about the refreshments
because if the Merlot's run out already
there's going to be trouble.
I read last, as the rest have somewhere to go,
and because there's swearing in mine.
What do they think I am, a token Scotsman,
some kind of caricature?
I give a small, angry stagger.
Isn't it odd, I say to a total stranger,
the number of Scottish drunks
in TV Drama? Outraged, I spend
the rest of the night
teaching a woman in a wheelchair
the right way you say get tae fuck.

Via Sacre

Hugh McMillan

There's a road we walk just now,
fringed by pine and bright bloom.
It leads to a mountain baked by heat.
It's not a metaphor, this road,
but a road, badly paved and cracked by the sun,
and the flowers, though old with meaning –
oleander for youth, hibiscus for purity –
have not been planted as symbols
along the way, nor does the slope bear
in its clasp some marbled and radioactive ruin
to the Gods of love and change.
It's just an old road,
with a pool we use off one end.
Each time I trudge along it
I stop and think:
such things I've seen today!
My children grew another inch
and swam away.

Book Terrorist

Graham Fulton

I put books on the shelves
of bookshops when no one
is looking

when the assistant
is eagerly stacking
the creaking wood
with celebrity memoirs

I lift them out of
my book bag

slide them into
the right place

leave,
slowly

I don't want money

Someone someday
might find one
and take it to
the counter and say
Dear Mr and Mrs Bookshop
how much is this excellently dusty
slim volume of slim verse?

and they won't know,
or how it got there

Torched

Lesley Glaister

First thing, in our new place, we burn
the chicken hutch. Tinder dry and tarry in the breeze,

still, it doesn't want to catch. We offer petrol, throw it sticks
and Leo, really getting into it, hacks and kicks to make air gaps

till *WHOOMPH* great raging cockerels of flame come flocking out.

Backed off, we make uneasy jokes about spuds,
marshmallows and the neighbours' wash.

When the roof falls in an oily hen of smoke
ghosts up to scatter cinder feathers over us.

Christmas Baling

Jim Carruth

That wet year after the war took his son
the straw lay cut in the field for months
a testament in rows to a failed harvest.

On Christmas morning, the land frozen
he set to remove this very public haunting
so hitched up the baler in the open shed

and was soon parading back and forth.
The old machine shaking off its frost
spat out dank bales as unwanted presents.

Working this day a gift to himself,
lifting the burden of loss from the ground
clearing the way for the plough's promise.

J.M.W. Turner's
The Fighting Temeraire

Jim Carruth

Toddler, head a laden cargo of now
leads his granddad along rows of leeks

pulls him behind like a rusted prow
loses him in the babbling squall he speaks

leaves him a ghost of furrowed brow
beached where past and future meet.

narrow lane

Jim Carruth

He meets me in the lane at dusk
in my dung covered work clothes

and in ten seconds has labelled me.
I see it in his eyes, the tilt of his head

his judgement a stripping away
a narrowing back to what suits him

so he removes most of my education
my qualifications, my time abroad,

my enthusiasm for community
my thirst for classics and the arts

my concern for third world debt
and though I have not spoken

he leaves in me a modicum of words
clumsily phrased, crude and rare.

The Barrow and the Common Grave

Jim Carruth

Midwinter and the mood sub-zero
we keep our jackets on in the pub.

The whisky isn't helping him
or this week's banker's letter.

He moves through the rounds
from sad-eyed melancholy

to brooding premonition
We're going to hell in a handcart

His outburst to the pair of us,
silences the public bar.

He stares into his glass
ponders our destiny and laughs

Just picture it, us three,
a free hurl and a wee heat, cheers!

Two-Faced

Olive M Ritch

Tossed on the Pentland Firth, looking
north-south, a voice whispers:

Julianna? Who is she?
Mother? Wife? Daughter?

The undertow tugs at the child -
I see Skara Brae, Maeshowe,

the Standing Stones, and
all the stories I do not remember;

in the bright field beyond,
a combine-harvester

chanting its Latin prayer
as it spews out golden bales.

Wind-nipped-women
in their counting houses,

awaiting husbands – bannocks baked
ale brewed, and beds longing

for brute sweat, warm
henches, and a deep amen.

PUNK Fiddle

JIM FERGUSON

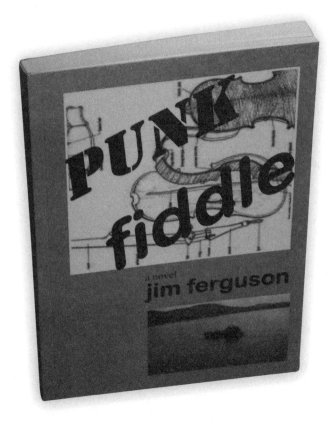

Debut novel by acclaimed Scottish poet, Jim Ferguson.

"Bobby is a 30 something Glaswegian who plays pool for money. He finds himself waking up in Edinburgh hospital and tries to piece his life back together. In doing so he uncovers the underbelly of post-industrial Scotland".

'...there's a lifetime of experience in Punk Fiddle, which is a cult novel in the making...'
Peter Burnett
Bella Caledonia

Get PUNK Fiddle at:
www.jimfergusonpoet.co.uk
AK Press and Amazon

WHIRLPOOL PRESS

Out There:
Call for Submissions

We're delighted to announce the call for submissions for Out There, a new anthology of LGBT writing from Scotland, edited by Zoë Strachan, to be published by Freight Books in September 2014.

We are seeking submissions of prose OR poetry by authors who identify as Scottish and lesbian, gay, bisexual or transgender.

A small fee will be paid for work included in the publication, and additional pieces will be published on the LGBT History Month Scotland website.

Guidelines:

You may send up to six poems (maximum 100 lines) OR one piece of prose of up to 4000 words.

Please include your name, address, email and telephone contact with your submission. Submissions should be emailed to **rguillory@freightdesign.co.uk**

Submissions should be sent as digital files: MS Word .doc or docx files, .rtf or .txt only. Hard copy submissions will not be accepted. PDFs should only be provided for poetry or prose with a concrete element.

There is no theme and work in any genre or form will be considered.

We regret that no feedback can be offered on unsuccessful submissions.

We gratefully acknowledge the support of LGBT History Month Cultural Commission Awards, the Royal Society of Edinburgh and Creative Scotland.

The deadline for submissions is 30th April 2014. Submissions submitted after this deadline will not be considered.

All work must be previously unpublished.

FREIGHT BOOKS **freightbooks.co.uk**

'I think if you ask anyone who's been divorced, they'll tell you that it's a wounding experience.'

Alan Bissett

Alan Bissett

The Gutter Interview: Alan Bissett

In this, a new regular feature, Gutter talks in-depth to Scottish writers about the breadth of their work.

Alan Bissett published his first novel, *Boyracers* in 2001. His second novel, *The Incredible Adam Spark* was published in 2005, followed by *Death of a Ladies' Man* in 2009. His fourth novel, *Pack Men*, a sequel to *Boyracers*, appeared in 2011, the same year Bissett won the Glenfiddich Spirit of Scotland Writer of the Year Award and was shortlisted for the Creative Scotland SMIT Scottish Book of the Year Award. Bissett is also a prolific playwright and performer with a string of sell-out one-man shows to his name including *The Moira Monologues*, *Turbo Folk*, nominated for a Critics Award for Theatre in Scotland (CATS), *The Ching Room* (for which lead Andy Clark also received CATS Award nomination for Best Actor), *The Red Hourglass* and *Ban this Filth!*. His script *The Shutdown* was made into a short film by director Adam Stafford and was winner of the Best Short Documentary Award at the San Francisco International Film Festival and selected at festivals worldwide. He regularly appears on radio and television and his performance piece *Vote Britain* has been viewed over 50 thousand times on Youtube.

Gutter: Let's talk about Boyracers, a real achievement for a very young man, having written it in your early twenties. How do you feel about the fact that it's still in print, making it part of a very select group of recent Scottish debuts – say for example the likes of Irvine Welsh's *Trainspotting* and Iain Banks's *The Wasp Factory* – novels that are still in print a decade after first publication?

AB: Well, it's had nothing like the sales of those books, but I think there is something to be said for that. You know, it's not a book that's a bestseller. It did alright at the time, it was Scottish Book of the Month in Waterstones which was great, and it's sold consistently over the years. I think partly because it appeals to young people, those between the age of about 14 and 17. You know, that period in upper secondary school when you're starting to get interested in books that are a wee bit edgier.

Gutter: How important do you think it is that *Boyracers* gives a voice to those that can be ignored within the wider canon, in terms of Scottish young people's experience?

AB: Yes, I think it definitely found a wee niche there. I mean, there are obvious precedents for *Boyracers*.

Gutter: Was *Trainspotting* an influence?

AB: There's no point denying that, it was a huge influence. I love *Trainspotting*, and *Trainspotting's* the book that gave me the confidence to try and write about my own culture, my own upbringing and my own language. That would never have happened otherwise. I was trying to write fantasy and horror, and it was literally like a sharp turn in the road. But what *Trainspotting* didn't do, and what I don't think any of the other

Scottish novels that I was reading at the time were doing, was A) deal with young people, and B) deal with those kids that are working class that aren't necessarily taking drugs, and in gangs and battering folk. They're very normal working-class kids, so the main thing in their lives is their mates, music, a good night out on Saturday and maybe going to the football. That's actually what working class life looks like for most males. I think the media has a distorting effect – the benefits cheat being the obvious example – where the life for people who are nearer the bottom of society is one of unending misery, abuse, alcoholism. These things exist, there's no point pretending they don't, and I do think that to some extent *Boyracers* looks at that when [Alvin] talks about his family, but I wanted to write about the sort of people that me and my mates were. That's what we were like; our main things in life were music and movies, and that novel hadn't been written. I think that's why it's found that little niche, because that's most people in Scotland. Most people aren't taking heroin.

'I think the media has a distorting effect – the benefits cheat being the obvious example.'

Gutter: On that point, literature can often be divided into the metropolitan and the provincial. Do you think that you started as a writer of provincial literature? Not in a pejorative sense, but in the sense of being interested in people on the fringes, who don't identify with the geographical centre. And do you think that's changed in your writing over the years?

AB: Yes, I do. The first two novels are about Falkirk, not even Falkirk, the same little bit of Falkirk, the same housing scheme. In a way, that provincialism is what *Boyracers* and *Adam Spark* are about, because you've got characters struggling with it. But there's also immense value in that. I think, looking at the sort of places that don't get written about, where people are just going about their daily lives, there's as much drama there. If you live in Falkirk, or you live in Orkney, or you live in Lewis, there's as much drama in your daily life as there is if you live in Brixton. And I think that's fine, that's perfectly valid. But I think inevitably I've moved on from a life in Falkirk, my life experiences have got broader, and also as a result of the first two books, I travelled a lot more. I saw all over Scotland because I was in book festivals and schools and libraries. Also I got chances to go abroad. So it's then hard to go back to writing about this little section of society that you did before, which I think is what *Pack Men* is about. *Pack Men* is about the struggle between the provincial and the metropolitan really. I mean, you can clearly see the difference between *Adam Spark* and *Death of a Ladies' Man* in terms of the canvas being wider. I think with the plays as well they're going a bit more widescreen in terms of Scotland. But I still find it hard to write about countries that aren't Scotland. So in that sense I'm still provincial.

Gutter: Why do you think that is? There'll undoubtedly have been commercial pressures from publishers to write a book that has more universal appeal. Why have you resisted that?

AB: Well, I don't know if it was so much a choice, it's just that that's what was written. You can only write the thing that wants to be written, and if the thing that wants to be written is set in Glasgow, the book is the boss.

Gutter: How much of it is also language?

AB: In at least three of those books Scots is quite important. Not so much in *Ladies' Man*, but significantly *Ladies' Man* is the one that sold the most, and certainly sold the most beyond Scotland, because it's written in English. It's set in the city and also within quite a middleclass strata of Glasgow. Glasgow's where I live now, and funnily enough, the next book that I want to write will have a rural setting, which is not something I've ever done before. Scotland's a country that I feel I know pretty well, and there's more value for me in exploring the different Scotlands that exist, because who else can do that? You know, someone who's studying on a creative writing course who has come over here from Spain or the US, the way they see Scotland is interesting and has value, but they can only ever see it from the point of view of an outsider. The people who live here and grew up here understand the country in a way that goes a lot deeper, so why wouldn't you write about that? I don't think I could go to Mexico or Canada or Nigeria or Czechoslovakia and write about these countries with anything like the depth that writers who grew up there could. So I think, well why bother? I could maybe write about the experience of being a Scot in Czechoslovakia, a Scot in Nigeria. That's interesting, but what is that contributing to

Nigerian literature? Probably fuck all.

Gutter: Do you feel a certain amount of responsibility as a Scottish writer to write about Scotland?

AB: Yes. Which isn't to say that every Scottish writer has to write about Scotland, you know, people write about what they write about. But I feel that responsibility.

Gutter: Where does that come from?

AB: I think it's maybe partly a class thing. I would imagine that if you asked most English working-class writers 'Do you feel a responsibility to write about the English working-class?' most of them would probably say 'Yes', because those are the values that I grew up with, and the culture that I grew up with, and I've got a lot of love for the community that I came from, and the family that I have. I don't see them being represented in media spaces with a great deal of accuracy, so I feel I owe it to them. You know, it's not like 'I am the voice of the Scottish working-class', that can sound a bit pious. It's more about my family and friends and the community that I came from, to say I owe it to them to make sure that their voices are out there and that they're being represented as part of our national culture.

Gutter: *The Incredible Adam Spark*, amongst many other things, is an examination of those who are dependent, and the extent to which they are funny, scary, sad, embarrassing. How much of that book is about Jude rather than Adam? What aspects of Adam were parts of yourself? What aspects of Jude were parts of yourself?

AB: I think it's probably as much about her as it is about him. As I started writing the book her character took on much more presence and prominence and a lot of the conflict was hers, because he often blithely just goes on his way, doing his own thing under his own steam, and Jude is the one who normally has to bear the consequences. So yes, I did feel that she was somebody who I found myself quite interested in writing about. Partly because, as you suggest, a certain aspect of her is myself. The pull of Jude away from Adam, knowing that she's got responsibilities there, and loyalties, but also feeling trapped by him, you know, I probably feel to a certain extent – or did at that time [I went to university]. Because you suddenly start to develop a different self, which jars a wee bit with the old self.

Gutter: Was there any intention that Adam be representative of a kind of fond caricature of working-class life, in the way that Shameless might be? In Jude's dilemma, he perhaps represents family and responsibility, in terms of his dependency. Do you think that was representative of your perception of that part of your life, a more innocent age?

AB: Yes, I think that's probably true. In a lot of ways I was quite naive when I was younger, so there's that straightforward aspect. I wasn't a worldly-wise young man. I didn't start drinking until I was 15, I didn't take drugs, I didn't lose my virginity until I was 19, so in some ways I was quite protected. But at the same time, I think there is a certain warmth about working-class culture when you're in it. It feels, to a certain extent, like a womb. Family's important to everybody, but for working-class people family's all they've got. You might not have a glittering career, you might not have the money to travel the world, so your family means an immense amount to you. I'm not saying that rich people don't love their families, but they've often got a lot more in their life in addition to their family. I think that, when I left that, to essentially chart out a course into the middle-class, I did feel a bit exposed. Suddenly you're confronted with values that aren't necessarily your own and you feel a little bit out of the womb, and that brings its own experiences and its own values and its own adventures. That there was an innocent part of me that was lost, left behind, my roots, that stands as an analogy. And I think that, since then, there's been an effort to get back to them.

'There is a certain warmth about working-class culture when you're in it.'

Gutter: Different writers unlock their fictions in different ways, whether that be via sense of place, a sense of location that stimulates the narrative, a final scene, for others it's a moral dilemma. To what extent is voice at the heart of what you do?

AB: I would say it's squarely at the heart of it. The writers that I've responded to most as a reader are the ones that have had a strong voice, almost unique. You can't mistake James Kelman's voice for anybody else, or Liz Lochhead's voice, or Bret Easton Ellis's.

AB: Why do you think that is? Do you think it's an inherent musicality in your approach or is it because you grew up in a household where there was a lot of talk?

AB: Yes, that's for sure. My family, and

extended family, are all big talkers. It wasn't a silent household by any means. So there's that aspect, but also there's a direct correlation, I think, between voice and the emotions that you attach to that voice, and so whenever I find myself speaking to a member of the Scottish working-class, there's a familiarity and a rhythm, and a persona change, actually, that comes with that, when I feel quite comfortable, because that's where I grew up. But also I think that it brings a whole culture and a whole set of politics with it, that you're not conscious of when you're young. Once you get older, and you do a bit more reading, you realise that voice is always political, it can't not be. Even if I'm writing in Standard English I still think the rhythm of it and the sound of it and the way that the words move through my mind unlocks character. So in something like *Death of a Ladies' Man,* there's a lot of fizz and pop and crackle in the language because that's what [Charlie] is like inside, in the same way that if you take a writer like Bret Easton Ellis, his language is dead and naturalistic and flat on purpose, reflecting the inner lives of his characters.

I don't know if voice is 'the' thing, and I don't know if it's the thing that gets everything started, because like you say, you can have a scene or even a title that appears to you and the story goes with that title. All these things contribute, but [I do believe] voice will ultimately dictate the success of the book.

Gutter: Do you think your enjoyment of working with voice and patterns of speech is one of the reasons that your transition into theatre has been so successful? Was that a conscious evaluation that you made, in terms

of 'I enjoy writing dialogue so therefore...'?

AB: I think it was more intuitive than conscious, as most creativity is. The way it developed was when I write a novel I have to read from it aloud at book festivals, schools. There was a strong verbal element there, as we've discussed. So the performances tended to be quite heightened, to the extent that it was half-theatre, really. I'm just holding a book. After many years of doing that, I thought, 'well, I've memorised this passage, I'll just deliver it'. Once I started doing that, I was into dramatic monologue. So it just seemed like a natural step to do it. I felt like I'd been doing theatre all along on the fly.

Also, it's nice to have something to offset the fiction with, because novels are long, lengthy, laborious things. It's like carrying a house around on your back for three years. At the end of it you're glad you've done it, but it's exhausting. I wanted a writing experience that was a bit fresher and zippier than that, and that's theatre.

'Novels are long, lengthy, laborious things.'

Gutter: What are your relationships like with your parents? Who would you say your dominant relationship was with?

AB: I was much closer to my mother. My dad and I have a good relationship, but he worked away a lot when I was young. That was just the way of it, so I just spent much more time with my mum, and my mum was the sort of person who was all about her kids.

My dad's very staid, he's a working man. His mind is quite linear, and that's not any discredit to him, that's just the way he thinks. Whereas my mum was far more emotional and passionate and open and friendly. She was, and always has been, a very dependable presence in my life, and I would say I probably inherited her emotional side. Which is not to say that women are more emotional than men. It's that Scottish working-class men hold onto their shit, Scottish working-class women don't, they let it out. I come from a family of 'letter-outers'.

Gutter: Were you surprised, to some extent as a relative newbie to performance in theatre, at the critical audience reception to *The Ching Room* and *The Moira Monologues*?

AB: No, because they were good plays and I knew they were good plays but obviously you can never predict to an exact extent how people are going to react to them, but I had confidence in them. You know, I felt the writing was strong enough and the performance was strong enough. I think the one that really took me off guard was *Moira* because, like I say, I had faith in the writing and the character, but the real risk was me performing as Moira, because I knew if I gave it to an actress they would do a great job with it. But the real risk was me. Firstly, as a novelist rather than a performer and, secondly, as a man playing a woman. That was the one I was quite worried about. That was the furthest, at that point, that I'd ever gone outside my comfort zone, and that changed everything, because I remember when it was on at the AyeWrite! Festival, which was its first showing, there was a big audience – about 250 people – and I think most of them were there to see me falling on my arse, and I was aware of that. There

was a curiosity factor for a lot of people, so I'm really glad that turned out the way it did, and something about the character struck a chord with a lot of people. After that I could go where I liked.

'I think most of them were there to see me falling on my arse'

Gutter: For you, how important is that risk-taking element? Is there something that compels you to constantly go further, to achieve more and to push yourself? When some writers are successful, they need to repeat that success again and again.

AB: I want to find out what I'm capable of, and it's very feasible that at some point I'll fail. I'll do a play or a novel that will land with a thud, and I'll have got it wrong because I risked something.

Gutter: A writer can make a large amount of money writing for television. Is that something in the back of your mind, to tick off the list at some point?

AB: Yes, and in fact I am writing for television. Well, in a way. *The Moira Monologues* were bought by the BBC, so BBC Scotland are trying to develop it, and obviously there's all sorts of hoops they have to go through in terms of getting it past the powers that be down South, and if you want to start talking about Scottish culture and independence, that's interesting. But we certainly hope to make it. I've written a pilot episode, and a screenplay for *Boyracers*. These are things I would like to do, partly because they pay more, and financial stability does help, but also partly because I want to write them. There's a creative challenge in that, and I think *Moira* would make a great TV character.

Gutter: One area that you're less involved in is short fiction. Is there a particular reason for that? Is it the lack of attention that short stories get, the media more interested in the bigger things, or is it more to do with the nature of short story writing; does it not attract you as much?

AB: I think there're probably various answers to that. When I was younger I wrote a lot of short stories. That's how I came through, that's how any writer comes through. So even before *Boyracers* I had been shortlisted for the Macallan [Short Story Competition] a couple of times, which was really where I broke in. *Boyracers* is much more visible now, but that really excited me back then, and it's where you're learning. You know, that's where you learn about voice and structure and character.

Gutter: Did *The Shutdown* start life as a short story?

AB: Yes, it did. Well, not as a short story because it's not fiction. A short biographical piece. It started off as prose and then Adam Stafford [musician and formerly lead singer with band Y'All is Fantasy Island] went away and put some images to it, and I was like, 'Knock yourself out, mate,' and then before I know it it's winning film festivals all over the world, I don't even feel like that was anything I did. I think Adam can take the credit for that. I remember asking Iain Banks, when I was a much younger writer, why he never wrote short stories, and he said 'because I'm writing novels.' He looked at me like, 'Is it not obvious?'

I said 'Do you never feel the need to do it?' He replied, 'Well, any ideas I get go into a novel.' Maybe that's why Banks has these big, rangy novels in which he's chucked everything in. I think that's what happens, the main thing takes over, and I don't want to talk about the novel as though it's a superior form, it's a different form, but it takes a lot more out of you than a short story does. So I do think I've neglected the short story over the years, but if I'm being quite honest, I don't think I'm a great short story writer. You know, I think I can hold my own, but I don't think I'll ever be talked about as one of the great short story writers of Scottish literature [laughs]. Like I say, you go with your strengths.

Gutter: *Adam Spark* was written at quite a difficult time in your life. Your marriage was breaking up. Did that have more influence on *Ladies' Man* as a book? Did the experiences of going through a major relationship breakup – although you were young at the time – did that influence *Adam Spark* at all?

AB: Yes.

Gutter: Did you feel more able to write about those feelings when more time had elapsed and *Ladies' Man* was underway?

AB: Well *Adam Spark* was written while it was happening, and I think to a certain extent that conflict between Adam and Jude, and Jude's the one saying, 'Should I stay or should I go?' These are things that are reflected in any marriage that's breaking up. So inevitably that angst went into those characters and *Ladies' Man* is about the aftermath really, because the flaw, the hairline crack that runs through Charlie's personality is that he's never got over his divorce –

obviously people get over their divorce, I'm over my divorce, right – but there's a residue that lasts for quite a few years and *Ladies' Man* was written in that period. I think if you ask anyone who's been divorced, they'll tell you that it's a wounding experience, you know? It's almost like a Masonic handshake, for quite a while after, you'll meet somebody at a party, in a club or whatever, and the fact that you're divorced comes up in conversation, and BOOF you're straight in. It's like 'Oh, how was it for you?' ...'Well, it was fucking terrible'. It's almost like you see the world through different eyes. Inevitably that's going to come out in the writing, and it came out in *Ladies' Man*.

'I think if you ask anyone who's been divorced, they'll tell you that it's a wounding experience'

Gutter: As a third novel, *Ladies' Man* was both a creative risk but also a big leap forward in your writing, in terms of ambition and complexity. How much of that was intention and increasing confidence, and how much down to having just changed personally since the first two novels?

AB: I think *Ladies' Man* was the book that it was because I was a different person. You know, that fault line had become quite large by that point, so I couldn't write about the world in as innocent a way as I did in the first two books. In *Boyracers* and *Adam Spark*, there is a lot of innocence there, there's a lot of naivety, although there's darkness as well. But in *Ladies' Man* there is no innocence, it's a darker world.

'In *Ladies Man* there is no innocence, it's a darker world.'

Gutter: In *Pack Men* you return to explore the idea of the divided self, both in terms of good versus evil, and also working-class versus middle-class consciousness. What drew you back to those themes that are also apparent in *Death of a Ladies' Man*? And why did you choose Rangers, football and sectarianism as a subject? Was it connected? Obviously Charlie Bain is an extreme character. Were you also attracted to the extremity of that particular culture?

AB: Yes, I think I am attracted to extremes. You know, Adam Spark in a way is an extreme character, Charlie Bain is, and the Rangers element is. These extremes in society – Andrea Dworkin, you know what I mean? The further out there people go, often it's, 'Oh, what's that experience like, being that far into whatever you're into?'

I think the fault lines in society are very interesting, so are the fault lines of class, the fault lines of gender. The fault lines of the sectarian divide somewhere like Glasgow are really interesting because where you've got those divides you've got tension, and where you've got tension you've got a story. *Pack Men* combines all of those things, because you've got Alvin in between working-class and middle-class, Falkirk and Edinburgh. He's in between sort of gay and straight, he doesn't know, and then you've got him plonked down in this quite extreme situation where those elements are in conflict with the environment. And he's also attracted to Rangers because that's where his mates are, but at the same time he's repelled by a lot of it. So yes, I think that's what that book's about. Also the sectarian divide hasn't really been written about that much, I mean think about how prevalent it is in Scottish social discourse, you know, the presence of the Old Firm. It's massive, and it's hardly ever been addressed – well only tangentially here and there.

I thought 'Let's get in about it', and that was a risk, because I had no idea how Rangers fans would react to that. Luckily the book wasn't such a huge success that it's on the bookshelf of every Rangers fan in the land [laughs].

Gutter: Why do you think that is? I think it represents a continued development in your craft and is different [to the others] and continues your development as a writer. It is a great book. Why do you think it hasn't had as much attention as your other books?

AB: I think there's a very straightforward reason. When the paperback of *Pack Men* was published, Headline had closed their Scottish list and *Pack Men* was on that list. So the trade paperback came out, it got great reviews, people were talking about it, and I was like, 'Right, here we go!' and then in between the trade paperback and the mass market paperback coming out Headline's Scottish list closed and I think it just got forgotten. Although, that said, it's the first book of mine that has ever been reviewed in *The Guardian* and it was shortlisted for the Scottish Mortgage and Investment Trust and I did win the Glenfiddich Scottish Writer of the Year on the back of it. So it did have effects, but the book itself kind of got lost.

Gutter: Clearly on the other side of Glasgow, books are a big part of that culture. The Celtic side. There've been a lot of very successful Celtic books, non-fiction and even fiction.

AB: There's a more literary culture around Celtic. I think that's fair to say, that there's always been a bit more of an intellectual weight to the way that club has been written about.

Gutter: Why do you think that is?

AB: Because Celtic historically is more associated with political radicalism, left-wing values, links to the Labour Party, Irish Republicanism. It's not to say there's not a troglodyte element to the Celtic support, of course there is. I find myself uncomfortable hearing songs sung in support of the IRA, I'm not defending that, but because there's a certain romanticism, because Celtic are associated with the underdog, that brings up more of an intellectual and artistic kind of support. I think because Rangers are associated traditionally with right-wing politics, monarchism, unionism, you know, the empire, that seems to have less intellectual credibility, and to a certain extent I think that's fair. But that's not to say that everyone who supports Rangers is thick, that's not to say that there can't be a fascinating discourse around those elements of Rangers, and actually that's what the book that's coming out this year is attempting to address [an anthology of essays by Rangers fans for and against independence to be published by Luath, edited by Alan Bissett]. You *can* talk about the issues surrounding Rangers in an intelligent way. Even the people in the book who I disagree with, and the people who I'm arguing with, I can still see there's a certain intellectual rigour about what they're saying, even if I disagree with their politics.

Gutter: There are very strong parallels between *Ladies' Man* and *Pack Men* in terms of the focus on a character who, to some extent, becomes discombobulated, examining the fault lines that exist in their personality. You take them on a journey to a place where they lose their identity and, in losing their identity, they find themselves or find part of themselves that was lost. What's the attraction of that kind of letting go, or of taking a character to the absolute inner depths of their psyche?

AB: If there is something that connects all four of those books it's a character who by the end has crashed, because it's very difficult to sustain a narrative in which the main character doesn't go through some sort of psychological crisis. I think sometimes you see that in genre fiction, not to be too elitist or anything like that, but genre fiction is about the story – characters are there too – but there are certain machinations that they are the agency in resolving. It's not about their psychological turmoil, and I think one of the strengths of the literary novel – and genre fiction has its strengths, story being one of them actually, which I think sometimes literary fiction can neglect – but one of the strengths of literary fiction is that you do feel the depth of the character more keenly.

Gutter: Having dealt with class in *Boyracers* and *Adam Spark,* and *Pack Men* in particular, and in *The Moira Monologues* as well, was *Ban this Filth!* a continuation of the themes of *Ladies' Man,* in terms of the frailties of masculinity? What draws you to masculinity as a theme?

AB: In attempting to understand masculinity you're attempting to understand your own condition. In the same way when you're out of your class, you're trying to make sense of it all. All of us, to a certain extent, are a construct, you know. We get certain values imprinted on us when we're young and we don't realise it's happening and we just accept them as natural and that's the same for any kind of identity. So masculinity – men are born with a penis, so obviously that sets them apart – but that question which has perennially haunted feminism: 'to what extent are male and female traits natural and to what extent are they cultural?' That's a really fascinating question, and so I want to go back and make sense of how I became 'male', if you like. That's there in *Boyracers* as well I think, definitely in *Ladies' Man*.

'All of us, to a certain extent, are a construct'

Gutter: In *Ban this Filth!* there's an ambiguity in that you adopt both male and female personas. Is that an important part of looking at gender and orientation?

AB: Yes, that's right, definitely. And I think with *Ban this Filth!,* what I hadn't done – I mean I'd always looked at things through the lens of being male, you know 'what's my take on being male?', because I am male. But what I tried to do was then look at it through the eyes of feminism. So that's looking at the same condition from the other side, and trying as far as I could to empathise with women's experience of men. And so who's the most extreme example of that?

Andrea Dworkin. She's the furthest point of feminism, so let's go there, and once I get there, let's turn around and look at men from that point of view. Once you start to buy into her world view, it's a pretty ugly picture. Now obviously that's only one view.

'What I tried to do was then look at it through the eyes of feminism.'

Gutter: It's also a something of a love letter to her as well. There's a very conciliatory tone, and at no point does it feel like you're having a go.

AB: No, and actually, even before the play came out, there was a real danger of a huge feminist backlash. I was worried about it for a while there because I was getting it from both sides. The sort of sex-positive feminists, who are about sex workers rights and all that kind of stuff, they thought that I was doing a hatchet job, and that then got incorporated and became part of the tension of the show. But then, about two weeks before the show came out, during advanced publicity for it, the other side of feminism got a hold of it and thought I was out to destroy Dworkin, and questioned my right to even represent her on stage. It's like 'how dare you'. They were saying things like, 'Oh, would you black up to play Malcolm X?' And to be honest, there was a part of me thinking, 'Well, maybe I would!' If I thought it could be creatively justified. I realised that there was a fundamental difference in the way that they saw Andrea Dworkin and the way that I saw her. For them, she was like a Christ figure, and I was blaspheming. I had

to just let the piece speak for itself. Once the piece had been seen it was clear that I wasn't out to take her on. But I wanted to try and interrogate – this will sound like the most pretentious sentence I've ever said – interrogate masculinity with the most extreme prejudice – to borrow that phrase from *Apocalypse Now*, to terminate men with extreme prejudice. Yeah, that was taking *Ladies' Man* to its furthest possible extreme.

Gutter: How much of *Ban this Filth!* and *Ladies' Man* is a response to your childhood, and what sounds like quite a matriarchy that you grew up in, and how much of it is more of a response to people today saying that masculinity is in crisis?

AB: I don't think masculinity is in crisis. You know, some men obviously are capable of empathising with women, even your sexists are capable of a form of love. I don't think men see the invisible structures of privilege that women see men having. Why would they? They're invisible. You know, people who experience privilege never think they're privileged. It's like if you ask somebody who's rich, 'you're loaded, aren't you?' they'll always go 'Oh well, I do okay', because they're comparing themselves to their mate who's a billionaire. So I think it would be actually much more useful for society if masculinity was in crisis. *Ban this Filth!* does directly flow out of my childhood, being brought up by women, well by a particular woman, my mother, but all the major influences in my young life were female. So I think it's partly exploring that.

Gutter: Do you have a sense of guilt about being male, in terms of that privilege you've just mentioned? Has *Ban This Filth!*

been a response to an increasing awareness of male privilege?

AB: Yes, for sure, it is, and to a certain extent you can't escape it because you're still male, and the benefits that come your way from being male, often you want to take advantage of. So it's a fight between your conditioning and your intellect and your empathy. I think, if you are a man who's awake to these things, then there's going to be a conflict, because you sometimes can't help but act male. You're on a stag weekend, you end up in a lap-dancing bar, you're not going to be the guy standing outside saying 'I disapprove of this', because your mates will hate you. So you get on with it. But, at the same time, I think society is getting more misogynist. It's also getting more feminist because there has been a feminist resurrection in the last couple of years. But that's because society has been getting more misogynist. You can ask young people about Miley Cyrus and Robin Thicke, and boom, they'll go on a half-hour monologue and to a certain extent these things were always in society, but I think pornography has changed the game in a lot of ways. I think in a lot of ways it's reconfiguring sexuality, in ways that we haven't caught up with yet. So I wanted to look at all of those things.

Gutter: Has the fact that your long-term partner, Kirstin Innes, is a feminist writer influenced your position?

AB: It's definitely been influenced. My last partner was a feminist, Kirstin's a feminist, and so inevitably that's going to feed in, because she'll challenge things I say, if she thinks what I'm saying has a sexism that I'm not aware of. She's got various things to say,

and also her writing has got strong feminist themes in it, and I'm interested in her writing, so yeah that does affect things. It's like being in a relationship with a vegetarian. To a certain extent you have to become a vegetarian because otherwise there'd be an irreconcilable difference there. So, yes, having a feminist partner definitely makes you a lot more sensitive to these things.

Gutter: There's often a sense in your writing that you feel that the dice are stacked against children growing up in working class communities, that people are unable to reach their full potential if they're born into one particular class. How much of your recent high-profile activity in politics, in terms of the independence debate, comes out of that sense of injustice?

AB: Directly. I found a political consciousness through literature, or a class consciousness, a Scottish consciousness. These things came through reading because when I started reading Irvine Welsh or James Kelman or Tom Leonard or Liz Lochhead, certain aspects of it chimed with my own experience. I'd never encountered those issues in literature before. Growing up you presume that literature should be written about other places, anywhere but Scotland, because why would you want to write or read about Scotland? Then you discover something that's written in the way you speak about the bit of ground that you have. It's actually immensely powerful and so you become aware of the ways in which your culture and your class are misrepresented, and you start to develop a much fuller, more 3D version of a culture that you had missed. Most of us grew up consuming Hollywood films or novels that are about detectives. Even though those novels are set in Scotland, it's often a very reductionist element of Scotland, which is simply about the criminal elements.

I sometimes worry that fiction which is about the everyday reality of people's lives is overlooked, and I think it's then harder for people to develop a sense of political consciousness which stands in opposition to the status quo because most mainstream culture confirms the status quo and that's not an accident.

***

'You become aware of the ways in which your culture and your class are misrepresented'

***

I became political because I was reading stuff that was scratching beyond the surface of the status quo, and so that's then the stuff that you want to write, and that then naturally becomes your politics. Now the politics has happened in the same way that the performance happened, it's just organic, it's just a sideways move. So somebody will say 'What's your opinion on this?' and, without even knowing it, you've got an opinion, and then that opinion becomes public so more people ask you to comment, and before you know it you've got a name for speaking up about politics. But also I do think that what we're going through at the moment is seismic. You know, what Scotland is going through at the moment is momentous, and I would be amazed if there were writers who didn't have an opinion on that. I'd find it difficult to take them seriously. It's like, well, are we just entertainers? You know, are we just here

to tap dance? No, we're people and people have political opinions.

***

'But also I do think that what we're going through at the moment is seismic.'

***

Gutter: Do you think that kind of direct activism gives you an opportunity to say things that you can't say in fiction?

AB: Yes, I would agree with that. I think you can get away with it in poetry easier, because political poetry, you know, it can be that concise. But with fiction, fiction explores the complexities of things. It would be very difficult to write a pro-yes novel.

Gutter: Was *Ladies' Man* a more political novel in its earlier stages?

AB: Yes, it was. But I think the politics in novels have to emerge by stealth. They come out from the dynamic between the characters. Possibly the only ones I can think of that are straightforwardly political, and still succeed, are things like *Animal Farm*, you know, *1984*, in which there's a clear political message.

Gutter: But they're effectively allegorical?

AB: They're allegorical. We don't really believe in the psychological reality of anybody in those books. Even Winston Smith to a certain extent is a cipher for resistance. Whereas if you look at a novel like, say, *The Grapes of Wrath,* which is still political, but has much more complexity and depth, you're under no illusions at the end of that that the Great Depression was caused by the rich. But it's not a manifesto. So I think, in fiction, it's harder to do that, which I think is why I'll make non-fiction statements and write essays and speeches where I can be unambiguous. But I will write a novel which deals with what we're going through at the moment, but it won't be a tub thumper. If you look at the plays that I've written, *Turbo Folk* and *The Moira Monologues* are both anti-nationalist plays – specifically anti-Scottish nationalist. Moira has a powerful speech at the end in which she condemns the whole idea of Scottish independence, and I think that's fine. You know, it makes sense for her. But something like the play that I'm going to be doing this year at the Fringe is explicitly a pro-yes play, and is campaigning for 'yes', and doing so in an entertaining way.

I think if you're any kind of writer of value you can explore the complexities. If you read a Kelman novel, he's got a reputation for being a sort of angry bruiser, but there's so much tenderness and sympathy and softness in a Kelman novel, they're not campaigning for anything. But if you read his essays, it's 'bam!' You know?

Gutter: Are you in a position to talk about what the next novel is going to be about?

AB: Yes, I haven't started writing it because I think there's no point until we know what the result of the referendum's going to be, because the Scotland that exists now, either way, isn't going to be the Scotland that exists after September. The country will feel profoundly different either way. So there's no point in me putting in eight months' worth of work, presuming that it's going to be a yes vote and it turns out to be a no vote. Or vice versa. So I have

to pause and wait and see the result, and to a certain extent I want to write about the aftermath, but obliquely. There's going to be a few firsts for me, it's going to be the first female protagonist in one of my novels, and she's going to be English because I think it's useful for me, as a Scot, and as a Scottish writer to look at Scotland from the point of view of the English. I've never done that. So she arrives in the Highlands with her family in the aftermath of the referendum – what's that going to be like? There's three firsts, it's a rural novel, it's a female novel and it's a novel about, to a certain extent, the English in Scotland. So that's what I can say about it just now. There will be themes that I've written about before that'll come up again, so as long as the execution is different. So that's what it's going to be.

NB: An extended version of this interview is available on the Gutter website.

The Bird Woman

Shaunagh Jones

Back then, I had everything I desired. All I wanted was to have a beautiful life. I wanted a car with a glossy red body like manicured nails, and to wear dry clean only fabrics that were weightless against my skin. In the daytime, I wanted to drink coffee with a mountain of frothed milk on top and at night, Kir Royales. I had a square-jawed boyfriend and a flat that was a short walk from the office where a job occupied me for seventeen hours a week. The bay windows in the living room overlooked a park with paint splash flowers and a cerulean stretch of water that children threw coins into. The floors were blond wood or rich coloured carpet and the walls were tastefully neutral. The rent was more than I could afford, but it was Ali's idea and I usually agreed with those.

He was older, more established. We moved in his furniture, plants with plumes of leaves and oddities he picked up on his travels: pottery from Central Asia and leather bound chests. Ali worked at an auctioneer and was sent on trips to seek out rare and expensive objects, but always managed to find something for himself. He would reel off the names of cities he'd visited, yet laughed at those who spent thousands on the objects he acquired for auction. I heard him on the phone speaking to clients and enthusing about their possessions, but once the call was finished, he'd tell me what he really thought. I'd pretend to agree, but really I was enchanted by the glossy brochures that lay around the house.

We took it in turns to make dinner. He bought shellfish from a nearby market and we sucked the insides from the alien-like bodies. The fridge was filled with bloody bags of meat from the butcher and squat bright vegetables. On Saturdays and Sundays, the front door stayed firmly latched and the unpacking was neglected. On Mondays, we stepped out into the busy streets, dazed and lost without each other.

The first time Ali was gone since we moved in, the bed was too empty. When I walked through the rooms my footsteps echoed. I thought about the other people in the building, only separated from me by a wall or a ceiling. The neighbours hadn't introduced themselves, but I'd heard their voices echoing in the hallway. I imagined a woman dressed in black and red, wearing patent heels, knocking on a hotel room door, and Ali, flustered, opening it. Then the image cut away, as if I'd switched off a television set and I stopped myself from picking up the phone to call him.

A noise made me sit up in the darkness. It was the muffled sound of tapping and scraping, coming from somewhere I couldn't identify. After a few minutes it stopped and I shut my eyes again, but I still couldn't sleep. All evening there'd been a smell hanging in the air. It had been noticeable, but not strong enough to bother me at first. I'd assumed it was coming from outside and couldn't place what it was although familiar in a way. I pulled the duvet over my head and I'd worry about it in the morning. It was gone by the time I woke up.

Ali returned from his trip, rumpled and with the plastic smell of aeroplane food clinging to his clothes. He kissed me in the doorway, closed-mouthed. I asked how it was and he told me fine, before presenting me with a gift. He'd been to Paris: city of designer shops and boutiques. The very name was like popping a cork from a champagne bottle. He handed me a selection of perfume samples from the airport and told me if there was one I liked he'd buy me the full size bottle.

The routine resumed. I enjoyed the weekdays that passed in fast forward and the languid weekends. It was some months before the smell reappeared. Ali started to notice it too and said he didn't know what it was. We opened the windows and lit candles in an attempt to exorcise it as it lingered for days at a time, faint but potent, before disappearing altogether. This was worse because it was difficult to identify. We called the landlord and knocked on neighbour's doors, but no one knew what it was, nor did it affect them. When we tried to ask the woman who lived in the flat next to ours she never answered our knocking, although we could hear her within. The family who inhabited the top floor told us not to bother. They rarely saw her, but when they did the woman scurried away, uninterested in even a perfunctory greeting. 'Bird lady, bird lady,' their little boy chanted before his parents shushed him.

I retreated back to our flat and unpacked the last of our possessions. We'd left them so long that puffs of dust rose up when I emptied the boxes. The two of us cleaned the rooms; I wanted to eliminate the possibility it was from us, although Ali told me it wasn't. He repeated it again and again, annoyed that I could think something ugly came from within our home.

The bedroom was dark and Ali's weight was stifling. It was late summer, and we had the windows open, not that it made a difference. I wanted them on, but Ali hinted that he wanted the lights switched off. His skin stuck to mine and I dug my nails into Ali's back to make him think I wasn't distracted.

It was there again and for the first time I realised that it was the smell of animal. Of something that lived in a forest amongst moss and trees and dirt; a creature that was only washed by rain. There was a creaking and I thought it must be the bed, but then I saw her standing in the corner. The woman dressed in red and black had her eyes, ringed with eyeliner, fixed on mine. Her posture was slightly stooped and two curved bones jutted out from rips in her chiffon blouse. A few tiny feathers were attached to them and I couldn't tell if her wings were newly grown or very old. Unblinking and wide, her gaze didn't waver as she watched us. I didn't make a noise, not wanting Ali to know I'd seen her. Her head twitched to one side as he groaned and rolled off me. Before he could see her, the woman silently left the room and a trail of matted black feathers floated down behind her.

Ali had been hiding the bird woman in our home. There were plenty of places she could go: the attic or the box room. When she'd had enough, she'd scurry back to her flat, knowing Ali was hers to return to whenever she wanted. She was something he could add to his collection of oddities. I remembered finding a handful of black feathers in his coat pocket a few weeks before and red blotches on his neck that looked like pinch marks.

When Ali spoke to me I still nodded as if I were listening intently. I kissed him, but it hurt to know why he'd become hesitant. My body was uninteresting to him; devoid of beautifully grotesque angles, twitches or feathers. When he ran his hand over my naked back I could tell he was searching for something. The bird woman had been in our bed. I knew from the way she looked at me that night, her eyes mocking, saying: 'I do it better.' Yet I acted as if nothing had changed.

I took my suitcase down from the attic, but didn't pack anything. It all seemed so strange; I wouldn't have believed she existed if I hadn't seen her myself. My Scandinavian father used to tell me folktales until I was probably too old for them. When I asked if he believed in these creatures, he said: 'There are things in this world that we can't ever be certain about.' I was reminded of his words when I found another clump of feathers down the side of the sofa.

She liked to play games. When Ali wasn't there, the bird woman would hide and then scratch and peck at the walls. I could hear her tearing at wallpaper, damaging wood. I looked for her, pleading that she stopped which just encouraged her. When I was sure I found her, I'd bang open a door and she was gone. All that remained was the faint beating of wings and the evidence of her vandalism. When Ali came home I showed him the tears and scores she created, pretending I didn't know what was causing it. He looked at me and said there was nothing there. He could see them though – there was a flicker of recognition across Ali's face before he composed his expression into one of concern.

Did he go and visit her? I pictured them entwined in her den of twigs and mud. Ali looked peaceful and had his arms wrapped around her, holding her fragile body close to his. Like he used to with me. When he was at home – occasions that were increasingly infrequent – he started to sleep on the living room or as far from me in the bed as possible. I covered the bird woman's work, splashing dark paint on white walls because that's all we had. As I painted I started to laugh because the way I'd wanted to live in a life-size doll's house seemed idiotic. I stood back from the wall, pleased that the evidence of her was gone.

I asked Ali what he thought of my handiwork and he didn't say anything for a while. Finally, he murmured: 'What have you done?' Then I saw what he did: bruises of blue across the walls, and flecks of paint dotted across the things he'd collected. I accused him of loving someone else, of leaving to be with her, of ruining everything. Why had he done it? When did it start? He couldn't answer my questions, but repeated sorry over and over again, trying to drown out the sound of my crying. It was as if he knew this moment was coming with his rehearsed apology and soap opera pained expression.

I started talking about the bird woman. She was so ugly; how could he love something so ugly? I told him to go and be with her bony body and forest scent. He could live in her nest amongst the leaves, broken eggshell and bird shit.

'What are you talking about, Nicole?' Ali said and the whole time she was tapping at the window. I could see that the baby fuzz on her wings had been replaced with spidery black feathers. He left me there on the floor, sobbing into the kilim rug.

I am standing at a window, looking out into the night shadowed countryside. My father is sitting in the corner of the room and the smoke from his pipe scents the room with woody tobacco. After Ali left, I bought a plane ticket. When my father greeted me at the door of house, he looked older than I remembered. We drank home-brewed beer and I told him the story of the bird woman. His arm snaked around my shoulder as I tried not to cry.

Sometimes, a bird lands at this window, the same one each time. It's large with sleek black feathers and eyes so dark I'm amazed it can see. It ruffles its feathers and caws at me. I bang the glass to try and shoo it away, but it isn't phased. I'd kill it if I could open the window wide enough. Instead, I stare at it and then watch as it flies away.

Beluga Song

J Johannesson Gaitán

To deserve the death of a Beluga whale, I began by no longer asking you how you'd slept. For so long I'd been exploring the beyond of your shoulder upon waking, bridging all these mornings, that by the time the whale arrived I was prepared for all kinds of new loves. How did we manage to pile up so many mornings? The flat, my flat, had become crowded.

To deserve her death I pulled the plug on your worries across the breakfast table. I would sit there trying to remember when we decided that you would move in, wondering if maybe I could veto it in retrospect.

'There's been a polar bear found in Norway. Starved,' you said. 'It had been wandering further and further south, looking for food.'

I wondered if I had eaten more healthily before you moved in, and I would stretch my upper body on the chair, trying to identify my spine deep within: the bony, original frame. The few evenings we both spent at home, free to pick up our choice of each other like neglected callings, I chose the opposite corner of the lounge. I worked hard to design a language it would take you too long to untangle. It was the one I spoke before you appeared, before you came plunging in belly first, into my flat, in between my before and after.

'It walked and walked,' you said. 'Looking for food. But there was no food left, obviously.'

You'd finished all the biscuits I'd bought to bring with me for work. They contained palm oil. That's why I'd chosen them, because I thought you would boycott them. I did all these things, and at the end of each day I looked at both our names on the front door.

A Beluga whale doesn't sing. Nothing it does is that simple. Its voice resembles that of a drunk in a BBC Christmas drama, so jolly you can hear the ale dripping off the tip of his hat. Or an opera prima donna who's just been told she'll be shot as soon as the curtains go down. She's only got that one aria left – they've cut her stay on earth short.

The first time I saw the whale was as a vertical sunrise, melting down over the rim of your shoulder, across the hall floor from the bathroom door. It was the first time we'd touched in two months, and it had come down with someone else's speed entirely. Like we were bicycles playing the nothing-to-lose-game of motorbikes. On my walk from the bus station this evening I'd been picking reasons – what we called each other, how you held your mugs, how many times a day you mentioned tuna . Then I had made decisions: who would move first, and where, and who would say it first, and who would make lists, and would this make any difference, and who would want the Patti Smith LP? Who would close the door last, and who would spit and who would swallow? The kernels.

When I opened the door, my keys still in the keyhole, you emerged from the kitchen. You were looking for your running shoes, wearing a pair of blue shorts which hung rather loosely around your waist. You didn't like those shorts. They made your legs look shrunken. Now, if I had known you only a little less; if how much I knew you was measured in a percentage of your body mass, and I knew you up to your forehead, then if I subtracted say half a percent of this – say I knew you up to your eyebrows – the shorts wouldn't have been a surprise. I stopped. It was this small percentage of you, once again made unknown, that made me kiss you as you were reaching for your shoes. It landed on your back.

Before we lived together, I used to say it reminded me of a whale's back, long and slender, pale, politely curved. Back then I said slightly cheesy, whimsical things like that. Back then, what reason did I have for knowing anything about polar animals? We were in the middle then – could go either way. What an easy place to be. Nobody is in the middle anymore. Not even the Equator, with the poles caving in and all.

It's a good thing we weren't in the bathtub. I have no doubt the whale would have landed nonetheless.

'Did you leave the bathroom light on?' I asked.

'No,' you said. 'Why?'

It was me facing the bathroom door and you couldn't see the respectful glow coming out. You moved your hand from my face down to my shoulder. You're a politician, a minor one, but devoted.

'Ok, I can tell you want to go turn it off. So go.'

In place of your fingers there was a centre, wavering in the draught. I said I needed to use the bathroom and closed the door behind me. There she was. Beluga had brought some freeloaders with her, small fish and shrimp splashing off the side of the tub and on to my bathroom carpet. There was a finger of algae drooping from the shower curtain, smelling rotten already but without any right to. It had only just landed.

In pictures Beluga whales are white. Surrounded by illusive ice and whatever water does to beauty, she would have looked clean. In my bathroom she was a mass of rubbery ghost-matter, her outline only just held together like dough in a cake tray. She was about four metres, her tail fin flapping despondently at the bathroom tiles above the sink, and the protruding forehead – which you would later tell me was called the 'melon' – squeezed under the bathtub tap. One of the fish was still twitching on the floor and, needing to do something, I hurried to pick it up and throw it in the direction of the bathtub. It bounced off the whale's back, making a sound like underwear waistbands. She was lying very still, with her head down as if counting to play hide and seek.

'There's no room for you here,' I gasped. 'You need to go, please. There's too many people here already.'

Then I felt bad, because that was what extinction was, a saying to someone that there wasn't room when they were obviously already there.

I couldn't tell you about the whale, so I went back out to having sex with you. We moved into the bedroom and for the next hour things were taken as they came. The floors didn't expand, though; we didn't gain more walls. So per laws of nature, some things must not have been taken in. Some must have been made to leave, or transformed into something that would never be the same.

At first I figured only I could see it. The next morning I woke up and you weren't in the bed. I heard the sound of the tap running in the bathroom. You had discovered her too. And while you bathed the whale you were listening to Patti Smith's *Horses*. It was like when we went for a walk in the Pentlands, our first summer, and you insisted on us coming back before seven so I could get the most out of my ideal working hours. You were good at seeing to others' needs. It made me feel like a terrible host.

What was left for me was to figure out what it ate. You were going to be interviewed by a journalist from *The Scotsman* that day, about the council's sustainability visions. Relatively, we live in the wilderness of the world, I'd heard you say, practicing in front of the mirror. We've got so much space we can sell it.

'Do wee politicians have taglines too?' I'd asked.

You wanted to be a big politician. Funny, thinking of space.

After you left I went in to check on the whale. The passenger fish were dried up on the bathroom mat like misbehaved leaves, and when I tried moving them they came apart in my fingers. It was only the smallest movement, but this upset her greatly and seaweed seasoned water flooded over the floor and over my naked feet. I reached for the shower curtain, which came off the rail, and as I fell I hit my knee against the hard enamel.

'I won't! Ok, I won't!' I muttered. 'I won't touch them!'

She calmed down a little. I left the fish where they were. I guessed she needed to mourn them. She was breathing very hungrily: like the air wasn't enough for her. I thought of the shrimp in the freezer. Now we were both providing something it couldn't do without.

When you came home I had grown an achy arm and a ridiculous water bill. Soaked from hip to kneecap, I waited for you in the doorway with the door open. I couldn't stand the sound of the keys I'd had copied for you.

'Feed something and it defecates,' I announced.

'What did you give her?' you asked.

'Shrimp. I did the research. She's also started singing.'

You pinched the wet fabric of my jeans as if checking the freshness of lettuce.

'They're called sea canaries,' you said. 'I checked at work. Research shows they try to imitate humans when in captivity.'

I knew you so well I didn't know where to look anymore. So I closed my eyes.

'I think it came from Canada,' you said. 'The fish looked like Arctic cod.'

Then the whale started singing again. It was excruciating, like someone pretending to laugh when they are in horrible pain. I put my hands over my ears. You pulled one of them down. I slapped it to my face again.

'You're hurting yourself. Come here.'

She sang louder, then she did that thing which sounds like sneezing. I had her in my bathtub and I had no idea why she did that, how she worked, nor how long this celebration was supposed to last. The cupboard behind the kitchen turned out to be the only place where the noise was slightly dulled, and you took me in there. There we stayed for the remaining hours.

She did sleep, and we only came out when she became quiet. The rest of the time we were restricted to the cupboard. Comforting, mourning, waking, had all become the same journey for me over the past two years. There were no differences between ways of touching anymore. With the song of the Beluga whale in the background, forcing me to stay locked in, little stops which I hadn't previously considered started to pop up along this treaded-down road that was your body. For so long I'd begun at your shoulder, turned left to shoulder blade, a corner around your hip to stomach and up against your chest. Dead end, not enough room. Begin again. After the whale barged in, this is what I found: where I slid down there was an elbow, and unfolding that there were ribs, sharpened because of all your late nights working, and all your running. You'd been running a lot lately.

'She sounds like she wants out,' I said.

'It's only a small bathtub.'

'Maybe I should move,' I said.

You shook your head. That had been the problem all along: my flat. Mine.

'When I was little I wanted to be a dolphin trainer,' I blurted out.

I'd never told you this because you were against zoos. And fair enough, a dolphin wasn't a whale. We might just have been talking about different things.

'What kind of dolphins?' you asked.

'Bottlenose. Movie dolphins, you know.'

I lay down next to you on my back, spread my legs up on the wall, wanting not out but up, and into: to be permeable.

To deserve her death we had to work hard. It is in our nature to allow things to happen, but then when you look back on it, sometimes it is possible to see all the open moments we could have escaped. We could have started throwing things out earlier. I could have made more room.

What was happening was death, slowly crawling not forwards but expanding. As Beluga got worse she seemed larger. We were beginning to stink, both of us, after not having had a bath in two days. And all the while, we touched. All the while, I never took the same route twice across your face. I went from anklebone to wrist and saw the unfamiliar in the corner of my eye. I stared at the crease where your bottom met your leg and couldn't understand what a body was really for, and who thought it could ever be attractive, and then it was beautiful, and then not. And all the while, the whale sang its drunken mantras.

The next evening, at some point between the time of day when you first moved your suitcases in to my home two years earlier, and the hour of the whale's arrival, Beluga died. When the silence had become so loud we couldn't possibly ignore it, you took yourself away from under my hands and got out of the cupboard.

A Floating Halfway House

Martin Cathcart Froden

Her family came down from the sheep-strewn hills. This, generations before she was born. They had been unable to settle a dispute over land after a supporting beam, weakened by weather and ill-advised carpentry, collapsed on top of four men, all with claims and wives and children. Her great-grandfather a swaddled lump of coughing pink then. Now they were stuck on the salt-sprayed rock, five walking bivalve molluscs clinging on for dear life. Housed on an inhospitable coast, with nets and tar and red raw fingers and a death wish just a fraction weaker than their natural buoyancy.

She was the youngest of three sisters, all named Maria, to her Mother's joy. When her Mother called for them she was unburdened and cleansed, a post-confessional feeling. The older sisters were quickly spoken for, negotiated over, married off. Soon wide-hipped with children, with button-nosed mushroom-babies, and more perpetually appearing at night. Our Maria was flirted with, patted, grabbed and even starry-eyed – on her back in the grass looking at the stars. At Orion's belt, as a man unbuckled his, to commence the grunting progress. But she was never spoken for. In those days someone like her wasn't.

Her Father wore a harried look, a ghost of himself. The wolves were collecting and one by one the heirlooms were carried out through their front door. In a daze she donned oilskins, yellow and too big – seawater always trapped in her upturns. Below deck she wore slippers, sheepskin, lined and warm. Her Mother's reluctant gift. An antidote to the mountains of mackerel eyes staring at her. To her Father's shame she sent money from cold ports far away, to his mixed pride she held her head high in the company of men and swore like the best of them, till she saw him standing on the dock welcoming her back to land and family.

From her hill-wandering forefathers she still kept her favourite smell, wet wool. The iron scent of a jumper pelted on by rain, torn and studded with thistles, gathered around her like an entourage around a princess. She brought knitting on board, the only trait of her sex other than her actual body. This Maria smelled of fish and guts and the acid droppings of crazed seagulls. As did everything else on the boat. She tried to subdue the smell of one animal with that of another. Gills for cloven hoofs.

The first two seasons out she brought the ship good luck. She worked hard. A sinewy, spine-strong girl. A whetted razor with a ponytail and a will to prove she was more equal than the others. To a point her gender didn't count, to a point her hair colour didn't either. As long as she worked twice as hard as everyone else, always agreed to the toughest shifts, highest waves and thinnest blankets. The only person she respected was the Captain, the only one she spoke to honestly was a small dark Portuguese man, ten years her senior, he too lost on the seas, her lover for the seasons out. When tiredness, storms, quotas permitted. After love she talked and he heard and looked at her downy copper triangle. Understood less than half of what she said, understood almost everything she meant.

The Captain's son had a keen eye for her but she was more interested in skate and sole than him. Tonne after tonne went past her eyes, and she paid it more attention than him. This he knew, this he felt, this he tried his best to change, but instead she went with the little swarthy bastard who couldn't even speak English properly, and who didn't do anything to deserve it. The son consoled himself with the Bible. She was meant for him and he had asked Him for her and thus she would slake his thirst, she would come to him through prostrations and prayer. He was relentless in his intonations of the old words.

Once, after, she had shared a cigarette with Raúl, a long-treasured, but awful, Paloma. A white bird, Noah's best friend, emblazoned on the pack. He was feeling sentimental, no doubt brought on by the cigarette. He had told her about Nazaré, his birthplace, and his Mother, long dead. About the chapel where he was confirmed, Capela da Memoria, built in 1182 to give thanks for a miracle. While hunting a white deer, the devil in disguise, the Virgin Mary saved a nobleman from falling off a cliff shrouded in mist.

Maria looked over his shoulder and thought she spotted a white deer. The Captain's son ducked back behind a tower of cages and went down to his bunk. To flick through pages crackling like maple leaves, putting the heavy, salt-stained tome on his lap again. Up above him the lovers talked about Vasco da Gama and Raúl's uncle the rosehip cultivator, and used the sea for an ashtray.

Walking home through the village she felt them looking at her. Curtains were hastily pulled, to hang slack again in the hope that she hadn't seen them. She who could spot a lobster – not yet red, but the violent purple black of volcanic rock – crawling on the bottom. These edible dinosaurs part of their livelihood. There was nothing wrong with her eyes. And there was nothing wrong with the money she was bringing home either.

Back on deck in the third season she cried but no one noticed in the rain. Salt water and cloud-sprung in a blend on her cheeks. With right hand pendulums the men sat, forfeiting sleep. Whisky to warm and whisky to stop the rolling of the ship and the rolling of the bowels. The very drunk could cry with her, they too sick of salt and sea, sick for loved ones and children only seen when the boat was dry docked. They showed her pictures of farms and families neglected. She showed them her saddest smile.

One of the men made his squeezebox groan like a tree falling over, then he played a polka he had learned when abroad, then he played a song his grandfather had taught him, the one about the two men about to hang. She cried as though one of the men was her fiancé. Then the fisherman made his instrument fart like a duchess (a quick squeal, like something coming out of a bottom attached to a stomach fed on tea and cream, on cakes and cucumber, so he said) and they cried with laughter. Their faces remained wet for all different reasons through his songs, his reels, his shanties until the bell tolled. Till it was time to haul in nets again. From the special black they hauled up creatures usually hidden in the recesses, in the silty caves. They were brought up to explode or bleed or asphyxiate and be thrown back, easy prey for the gulls and gannets, or to be gutted and put on ice. A fishing boat is a cold hell's antechamber. A floating half-way house: not wet, not dry, not sky, not sea, not land. Nothing really. Just a speck on the ocean, taking things from the sea, putting them on plates, putting nothing back apart from slime and death, and making the birds screech with happiness. The wheat of fishermen harvested in the night is a sharp, icy sheaf.

In her fourth season catches diminished, a matter quickly blamed on her. They should never have allowed a woman on board. The ship was a woman already, one was enough, everyone knew that, and now she had disturbed the balance. She with blood leaking out of her like the ship did when they were gutting fish, she whose body navigated after the moon, like the ship when tides kept them in or out, away from profit or away from home. The Captain apologised, said he didn't mind redheads or that she was a woman, and that he for one didn't believe in any of the old nonsense, but the men, always the men, the herd of men he was charged with, had been slow to accept her and now quick to turn on her. She could see his point surely, but he was sorry to see her go. Would help if he could. He asked her not to return once she had set foot on dry land again.

That evening the son caught Maria and the Portuguese man out on deck. As she walked back to her cabin he fell in next to her, begged her, said he would pay, told her it was her last night anyway, couldn't she just…? The more he pleaded the more she shook her head.

In despair he pulled down his trousers and tried to brush up against her, but it wouldn't stiffen and she laughed and he pushed her. He found a tool and swung at her in a fury, she laughed even more and he pushed even more. She fell into the sea and by the time he had put himself away it was too late to turn the boat around.

The next day they caught a record catch. Nets teeming with silver. When she was due to come on shift she was not in her place in the line. The lifeboats were counted, her belongings looked at, heads shook, her pay suspended. Raúl cried openly and the Captain radioed the Coastguard. With the weather conditions, the currents, the general depreciation of fishermen, it was sad, but no surprise. People go overboard, go under the surface, eventually. The son consoled himself with the story of Jonah. She had made a mockery of him and she had deserved it for being a harlot. The catch had been very, very big and his Father the Captain had been pleased. It had been an accident, but he was glad she was not there to show the mark the spanner had made in the back of her head.

A month later a wreath of flowers was dropped over the gunwale by a too-tired-to-sob-any-more Mother. The only way to pinpoint the unmarked watery grave. The fishermen all took off their headgear, one more reluctantly than the others, but at a glance from the Captain he retched with guilt. Acid sprayed into his gullet made his eyes well up in a convincing picture of grief.

At the same time Maria walked down the makeshift aisle, made from plastic seats, some matching, most not, in Raúl's uncle's garden. The seats were adorned with rosehip, thorns bred away years ago. On her head a wreath of flowers, white, like the sheep on those far away hills. Her veil hiding a spot where a scar will forever stop hair from growing. Her family is there. All two hundred generations of them: Bronze Age women, medieval plague victims, back-broken crofters, sheep farmers – but only one fisherwoman.

College St., Kolkata

Donal McLaughlin

(For Chriſtoph Simon)

May I tell you about my walk yeſterday? Before the memory pales? While we were ſtill ſtuck in traffic: the gaggle of yellow taxis. A guy 'showering' at a water hydrant, on the road side of the railings. The – drenched – clothes he'd been wearing hung over the railings to dry. The driver pulling in on a thoroughfare, lined solely with bookshops. A man's hand mouthing 'Some-thing to eat? Money for something to eat?' before we were out of the car even. The way the driver shook his head, the way the beggar scarpered. The *English Literature* bookshop, beyond a slanting tree-trunk. The firſt of: bookshop after bookshop after bookshop. Standard-sized (not: *ſtandardised*) shop-fronts, ſtacked full with books. More bookshop side-ſtreets beyond the mental traffic. The initial impression of chaos, yet the shops, often, are ſpecialiſts. An author, his translator and a bookseller, trying to read their driver. My 'Maybe, the idea is: we ſtroll around a bit – and return to the car once we're ready?' Amit suddenly appearing as we were ſtill taking our bearings. An initial short ſtroll from where we parked. Presidency College: part of the University now; the map has yet to be changed though. Hare School, like the Hindu School opposite: 'famous only for their hiſtory'. Arcades. Alcoves. 'Very English' ſteps, leading up to blue sky. To palm trees. Ahead: Saraswati. The goddess of learning – and of books and music – before blue and white drapes.

    Retracing our ſteps, to ſtart the walk proper. Across four, maybe, lanes of traffic: the famous INDIAN COFFEE HOUSE. 'Where intellectuals meet'. To its right: purple and yellow signs, screaming colour, fabrics, fashion. Its left: an unfinished 'book mall'; the flimsy bamboo scaffolding. Daring to cross an Indian road, *shepherded* by Amit. In the firſt side-ſtreet even: the bells & horns of tuk-tuks, rickshaws, tricycle carts, all wanting paſt. Tannoys. The appeals made by out-of-power Communiſts. SUCI. CUSI. Block capitals (white) on red, vertical banners. A second Saraswati. 'The only important goddess worshipped in winter'. Celebrated this weekend, then chucked into the Hooghly. A diſplay of books in Bengali. A hint of soft porn. Motorbikes – the lines of parked motorbikes. As I look through my viewfinder, the tricycle coming towards me. The driver and bike clearing me as I photograph the lane. The *FU-U-U-CK!* suppressed when the rear wheel hits me. The *SHIT!* that *does* escape. The shin that's fucking aching. Amit: 'Did *he* hit you?' Me (*reluctantly*): 'Yes.' Then: 'It's okay, I used to play football.' The checks and diamonds of pullovers, in twenty degrees Celsius. Drifting into a side-lane. The textbooks & ſtudy guides; the ſtacks of them. The guy with a phone to his ear: reading English, but ſpeaking Bengali. Books piled Aldi-ſtyle, so exposed, you fear rain. RAY BOOK CONCERN: its liſt of publications on huge purple boards. The guy at the bottom of my photo going from sullen to a big warm grin. Snack bars, next. Huge kettles

& teapots, the heavy-duty variety. Batter, sizzling in fat. Serious flames licking the bottom of something wok-shaped. A vendor, in the lotus position, shifting none of his local speciality. Oranges stacked in pyramids. A different angle on the book mall. The light blue buses, their orangey-yellow stripe. A conductor on the platform, his fan of folded banknotes. Guys nipping between buses, the *stacks* of brochures they shoulder. An older man, *pushing* his trike, his cube of paper shreds. Shop signs promising EVERY BOOK. Every *school* book, I reckon, for sure. *International* this, *international* that – from shabby-looking bases. BOOK VALLEY. A rash of letters after names. Letters, as in: qualifications. A poster, all in Bengali, but for one word of English. That *Sexologist* looking WANTED; like a Baader-Meinhof sidekick. The male arms round male shoulders of touchy-feely teens. Amit addressing only Urs now, as Rick and I take photos. A wizened old man in a tank top: (less than subtly) stopping to eavesdrop. The intense, critical scrutiny in the eyes behind his specs. A lad clocking my monitor, stubbornly invading my space to follow what's happening. A *deserted* lane, suddenly. Alleys, back lanes, yards, yet the discourse is always: *management*. Posters – here, too – promising GUIDANCE & SUCCESS. 'Effort is Our Promise. Results are Our Target.' More frequently now: hammer & sickle graffiti, a dark shade of red. Green cartoon flowers sprouting from fly posters. Parked, empty tricycle-carts. On the corner: two rows of gods, on seven painted tiles – 'to stop people urinating.' A stray dog nuzzling in un-bagged rubbish. The surprising (apparent) absence of rats. A guy on his hunkers, his trousers at his ankles. ENGLISH GRAMMAR & COMPOSITION – showcased. Bengali, otherwise. Few and far between, the odd hints of rain. An old dear peering down from her balcony, the sat dish over her shoulder. A gorgeous girl, squatting, *sweeping* the surrounding ground, until bikers, determined to tease her, point to my camera. The laughing smiles of the guys who made her flee. The local mosque, its green shutters. Peripheral vision: checking, always, where Amit is. Where Urs is, and Rick is, too. The smell, suddenly, of INK! Peering into a printer's, my zoom primed. Machines, Urs tells us, that go back to the forties. The paper: cut by hand. The shreds: collected. The mobile over the door

:

a lime
3 chilli peppers
a lime
3 chilli peppers
a lime
3 chilli peppers

:

Our speculation re: possible explanations. Pavement, suddenly: broken bits & pieces requiring careful steps. A quieter lane. The average age *younger*, maybe. A guy in red-and-white hoops climbing onto his saddle. The girl he – perhaps – works with; her supply of bright-pink jotters.

The 'electricity box', at head-height, that *isn't* what you think. 'It contains a television.' Trying to imagine a test match; the whole neighbourhood watching. Turning a corner: College Street up ahead again. On our way back to the car, clearly. The occasional person listening, still, to whatever Amit's saying.

Extract from the novel *Thicker Than Water*

Zoë Strachan

Bugger Rena, bugger the hotel, bugger Frank Gibson, bugger Frank Gibson's daughter, and bugger beef Wellington and pavlova for ninety. Bobby drops his speed before the schoolhouse. Doubtless Miss Kenyon is tucked up in her flannelette by now, but he doesn't want to take any chances. When he gets past Fenwick he kills the lights as well. It's a familiar enough route and the moon is out. He reaches for the glove compartment, feels the car veer across the road as his fingers stumble on the catch. Empty. Bugger Rena all over again. Wherever he planks a half-bottle, she finds it. The only place he can drink is the buggering hotel. She won't chide him in front of staff or customers.

Getting Marjorie Gibson's wedding is a coup, he has to admit. Rena aims high. Her campaign started a few months back with a nightcap on the house, and Bobby has been glad-handing the man ever since. And now, here he is driving to Glasgow at midnight with a fistful of coupons and a wallet of cash, to see a man about beef fillet and icing sugar.

Bobby comes from the city. Creeping up to it at night warms his blood and sends a tremor of threat down his spine. The tenement crush, the ninety degree angles, temptation and retribution behind every door. The first time he ran away to sea it was because the city was too small. Second time because it was too big. More chance of drowning there than in the Bay of Bengal. He'd been demobbed under a week when he had a vision. Rena, through the window of a furrier in Sauchiehall Street, trying on a musquash. A lily-white, fiery-haired beauty, set off by a gaggle of old women in tweeds and dark-rimmed spectacles. His cigarette burned down to his knuckles as he stood there and watched her turn this way, then that. The heavy fur of the collar brushing her jawline, the hem sweeping around her calves. All the while looking at the mirror rather than her audience of widows and spinsters, as though there was another world through the glass. He'd never seen anyone so self-possessed.

Bobby turns the headlamps on again when he approaches Newton Mearns. The main road is the danger for the black-marketeer. The police sit with binoculars at the hill at Waterside, or at least that's how Archie Gemmell got done. So kill your lights, Rena said. She hasn't done too badly herself. Round a dozen farms to sort out the eggs, butter and cream. When she got nearer the coast some of the farmers minded her from when she was a girl, awfy bonny on her bicycle, delivering newspapers and bread rolls from a sack. She wouldn't have known she was a looker back then, tall for her age at fourteen. She hardly knew when Bobby met her. Maybe that was the turning point, seeing herself as a woman in a fur coat, that day in a smart shop on Sauchiehall Street. She was with her mother and her Auntie Nell, he found out later. Nell knew the proprietress from before the war. She'd have got a good price on the coat. Nell's canny that way.

At Jamaica Bridge he feels his heart begin to pound. It isn't exactly the city that never sleeps but there are indications of wakefulness after hours. Figures in doorways, lights in windows, cars hiccupping at traffic lights. He could turn left, go straight ahead, ditch the motor and walk along the lane on the right. There's a door on the left. Ring the bell and when the grille opens say that Eva sent you. Which Eva? Eva upstairs. Climb steep steps, and it's through another door to candles and red plush banquettes. Neat'll be fine, just a drop of water in it. A brunette in the corner of your eye. Looks too good for a place like this but then there's theatre folk in, and all that comes with them. Buy her a drink, have another yourself. Chink every glass, fall for every line, right up until you're standing in front of the registrar hoping he won't come close enough to smell the whisky on your breath. Hoping he will. Anne wasn't ready to go straight, and Bobby was never the man to help her. Maybe that's why the city makes him uneasy. Even if it is where he first spotted Rena, his second wife, his saviour, with her milk-white skin.

'I don't want to hear her name and I don't want anyone to know about her. They're not going to think I'm second best,' Rena told him, and that is how it has been. Adieu, Anne; except she was already gone.

The only cures for thinking too much come out a bottle or between a woman's legs. Bobby would settle for the former, if there was somewhere to get a nip before the deal. Ah Christ, that'd be the end though, wouldn't it. He turns right at the lights, heads towards Bell Street. Beef fillet and icing sugar it is. But he'll be damned if he's driving straight home afterwards.

'Silverside?' By the time he finds the warehouse he is edgy and cocky. 'Come on Lou.'

'Top quality. The best.' Luigi Zambardi had a tough time when he was interned, or so they say. He's emerged from it tougher still.

'I don't care if it's fucking gold-plated,' Bobby says. 'It isn't fillet.'

Lou shrugs. 'There wasn't the quantity. You got your sugar.'

'And I paid you for it.' Bobby turns to leave. 'That'll have to do me.'

'Meat's been through the roof since it came off ration.'

'Aye well, it's not what I drove twenty miles in the dark for.'

'What am I meant to do with all this then?' Lou waves his arm over the table, three fruit boxes stuffed with packages of blood-spotted newspaper.

'Lou Zambardi at a loss? I don't believe it. But you'd better get that lot in a refrigerator or you'll be lucky to sell it for dog meat. Sayonara.'

Bobby walks away, nodding to Lou's nephew, who is loitering by the door. If he is there to provide muscle he doesn't look up to the job. Skin and bone, none of Lou's tanned sleekness. Sleek and sleekit. Bobby reaches in his pocket for his cigarettes, slips one from the pack. Whatever happens next, he can feel the tingle of whisky on his tongue.

'Hold on.'

Bobby stops, strikes a match. It fizzes into life and he touches it to the tip of his cigarette, inhales.

'I could do you a deal,' Lou says.

Bobby turns and smiles, palms open. 'Why didn't you say so?'

It is another lane he finds himself in, leading to another afterhours club. Immediate membership available, no card issued, strictly below board. Neat'll do fine love, just a drop of water in it. Bobby catches a glimpse of a woman with dark glossy hair, turns to look at her but it isn't Anne, how could it be? A pale shadow, powder gathering in the lines around her mouth, her crow's feet. On closer inspection, the hair is more than half hairpiece. She smiles at him, places a cigarette between her pinched lips to ask for a light, but he turns away, almost bumps into the blonde next to him at the bar, maybe not that much younger than the brunette but her eyes are brighter and she looks as if her lines come from laughing.

'Buy you a drink?' Just one, he tells himself, just one more and he's off, with the boot of his car stuffed with icing sugar, silverside and a case of champagne. French champagne.

'Port and lemon'd do the job,' she says.

Bobby nods to the barmaid. 'And have one yourself, love.'

'Of whom do I have the pleasure?' the blonde woman says.

'Bobby.'

'Thanks for the drink, Bobby.' She raises her glass. 'I'm Jean.'

Before he knows it he's telling her about the wedding, asking her if you can turn silverside into beef Wellington.

'Do I look like I learned cordon bleu?'

'You look like that actress, what's her name again...' He can't stop himself.

She laughs so that he can see a gold tooth flash at the back of her mouth. 'Oh aye, whatshername. I'm often told that.'

'I bet you are.' He downs his drink, hesitates. She pauses too, her glass halfway to her lips, as if time has stopped. Then her face breaks into that lovely smile again, except this time her eyes don't sparkle quite so much.

'Look love, I'm working. Either go back to your beef Wellington or...'

He thinks of Rena, one loose strawberry blonde curl falling over her forehead as she orchestrated the seating plan for the wedding. The linen is starched, the tables are set. And Frank Gibson is in the Rugby Club. Rena is smart. If Marjorie's wedding comes off it's just the beginning. Eleanor Anderson's engagement was in the paper last week, and they've heard terrible reports of Patricia Scott's twenty-first at the Foxbar. There's a gap, and the Ossington Hotel can elbow in to it. Those and such as those are nothing if not competitive.

'One for the road?' he says. He hadn't guessed Jean was working. A woman alone, dressed up and drinking in an afterhours bar? Naïve, he supposes, but maybe he has always been. Look at Anne. But Anne was turning over a new leaf, wasn't she.

Jean glances around the room. It's busy, for two on a Tuesday morning. He guesses she has other options and sure enough: 'You're wasting my time,' she says. 'Go home.' The old smile comes back, just for a split second, as she pats his arm. 'And take care.'

He nods. The banquettes here are green plush, and have seen better days, and the stairs lead up to the front door rather than down. He tips the sullen doorman as he leaves, remembering his first date with Rena. She thought he was someone, the way he tipped the cloakroom boy at the Grosvenor and slipped the musquash round her shoulders. And he thought she had money, not knowing about her mother's divorce. Rena's got class though. You can't buy that. Beef Wellington; steak pie by any other name.

Cloud descends over the moor on the drive home and what starts as mist soon congeals into dense fog. Or is it just the darkness, he can't tell. More than once he hits the verge, has to shift back on track. The danger is enough to numb his thoughts. No lights until Fenwick, just like Rena said. So how far is Fenwick? He's been driving three quarters of an hour, more. The year before last, three walkers got caught in a snowstorm on the moor. They walked and they walked, not able to see a foot in front of them, not knowing they were going round in circles. They walked until they had to sit down and rest, with the soft snow still falling all around. When they were found, they were ten yards from the main road. There is a memorial cross on the spot. Bobby peers through the windshield but he can't see a thing. No lights until Fenwick, she said. Well, maybe he's at Fenwick, or maybe it isn't worth the risk. But he keeps going in the thick grey darkness, edging forward what feels like an inch at a time.

Bang.

His chest hits the steering wheel and he slams on the brake, too late. He's hit the buggering fence. Deep breath. And again. Sit up. He prods around his ribs. Nothing broken. Worse things happen at sea. He barks a laugh then drags the gear into reverse, feels the wheels spin in mud.

'Come on.'

The axle whines, or is it the wheel bearings? He gives it a rest, tries again.

'Come on.'

The Austin lurches and he pushes it further, waiting for the back wheels to hit tarmac and grip. Christ, will he have to get out and push the thing? Another lurch and he takes his foot off the gas. He must be sideways on the road now, but the chances of anything coming up behind him are slim. Which way was he pointing? That way, must be that way. His hand hovers over the lights. As if there'd be polis out on a night like this. Don't take the chance. Keep going.

At last the fog begins to unravel into fine white threads. There's a light, up ahead and to the right. He leans on the brake. Slowly does it. Two lights, three. He is at snail's pace now. The lights resolve into a building. The farm at the Galston Road end. Nearly there. By the time he reaches Fenwick the moon is overhead again, almost full, but he switches on the headlamps anyway.

He parks in the back lane by the whisky bond, opens the boot. Knock, double knock, knock on the kitchen door and there's Rena, pinny over what she calls her chartreuse dress, her face in shadows.

'Don't leave the boxes on the ground. There's rats.' He pauses, and she squeezes his arm. 'All right?'

He nods, and begins carrying the meat through to the big refrigerator. Her hand has left a flour mark on his jacket.

'Leave it on the table,' Rena says. 'I'll put it away.'

He empties the boot, leaving the two crates of wine until last. Slinging one under each arm, he shoulders the door open. Rena has opened one of the packages of meat.

'What do you call this?' she says.

'Silverside. It's all I could get.'

'Have you been drinking?'

'No.'

'If I'd wanted silverside I'd have got it from the butcher.'

'Not at this price you wouldn't. That's the whole point.'

'And you'll explain to Frank Gibson why his fancy dinner's tough as an old boot? That's if we don't poison him by undercooking it...'

'It'll be wrapped in blasted pastry and Frank Gibson'll be three sheets to the wind by the time he eats it. Especially after we've warmed him up with this.'

He slams the boxes down on the table. The bottles chime against each other like church bells. A call to prayer. Rena tucks the newspaper back around the meat she's unwrapped and puts it away.

'Champagne,' Bobby says. 'Gratis. I made Lou throw it in to compensate for the meat. Look, it's French.'

She inspects the box. 'It's always French,' she says.

'Eh?'

'Champagne. It's always French.'

Rena, Rena. Bugger Frank Gibson, he wants to say, bugger staying up all night to make pastry, let's you and me crack one of these open and drink until we're giddy. He imagines her laughing, the way she laughed when he drove her back down the moor road after that first date. Hardly a drop of alcohol in wine, he told her, that's why they drink it all day over on the Continent. Tell me about Rome, she said, and he gave her a scrubbed-up version of Naples, added in the Coliseum and the Pope in a frock. Rena, let's drink champagne and run away to Rome. Would she have gone for it, ever? Ah well. That's why Rena has the edge, that's why she is his saviour.

The mole

Helen Addy

His nest of silver hair deserted,
unfastened buttons let him hover
in the dip of the throat.
His eyeless face
finds comfort in shadow,
but every swallow
brings him back to the light.
Lovers dig for him,
their lips filling his hollow bed
like pale worms mouthing
a blind particle of earth,
darkening with each bitter taste.

April

William Bonar

This morning a dotted line of geese
printed on dawn, a buzzard
spiralled the serrated edge of need.

Digital or analogue our time piece
unwinds. Spring's coming is hard.
Despite our gnawing, desires recede.

Hymn to Persephone

William Bonar

Seek my famine, I will wait for you
among leafless birks, in hermit cell.

Speak only of shapely things,
of tree and shade, kernel, pattern.

Caress my cropped, suckling head,
catch your breath on the pulsing barb,

scrape the corners of my empty kiſt,
green me, green me, green me!

I Love Him like an Oak Table

Marion McCready

so solid and Plato. His lips, two candles
lighting and lighting.
The chorus of my crab-claw tulips
bubbling, their red gowns floating
from the plaſtic vase.
The wine glasses drain from our wriſts
as he reſts like a tree trunk
curved into our high-backed, high-loved chairs.
Drink up, my love. Supper is over,
tomorrow the cock will crow.

On Benbulben

Charlie Gracie

Meadow Pipit

A swirl-chirp blurring above
the height of the mountain. Silence
blasts out below

Ancient

the chortle call of choughs
flickering out over peat hags
fairies in the bog-lit mountain

Yeats

In the green expanse of Sligo
a river wanders through
the footprints of ancient forts

Civil War

A step from Bulben to Wiskin
to something un-named
hands wrung, blood-saddened

Leaving

behind you, beyond the whins
a Council of Crags
in the softening sun

Blonde Woman with Sunglasses

Samuel Derrick Rosen

Sometimes everything becomes
as meaningless as a blonde woman with sunglasses.
Still, there is something reassuring
about the blonde woman with sunglasses,

as she sits there alien
to any regime,
while I build my new empire
of vanilla ice cream,
so quickly it melts, to a cipher supreme.

All spheres seem impenetrable
as this blonde woman with sunglasses.
Where do I know her from? A reality removed?
One the gods have forsook?
Or possibly from a picture in some pictureless book?

There is nothing here to romanticize,
no hell to imparadise, just an image gnawing
inside this spectral ordinariness, inside
this endless genesis waits a blonde woman with sunglasses.

Against a world of grain, against a simplicity
none dare explain, against the immeasurable
sits the blonde woman with sunglasses.

Emitting herself, below gravity and sun,
in the knowledge that everything
has already been done,
that nothing is ever contained in a day,
that one more metaphysicist shall kneel down to pray,

that the common man sleeps a great absence of time,
and that that in itself
is oddly sublime.

Sometimes everything becomes
as meaningless as a blonde woman with sunglasses.

My Man

Jim C Wilson

My man's a sweet man: he rises
at six (knowing my needs) and we stroll
the ornamental gardens. He shops
for me, prepares and serves my meals.
I have no vile or tedious chores
to perform. I'm fondled frequently –
and caressed just like a lover.

Today, as ever, I flashed my teeth
and popped out my long pink tongue.
Drops of saliva fell like jewels
on frosted grass as, panting and rapt,
I produced my steaming morning mass.
I howled in triumph, the act complete,
then turned to greet my lovely heap.

I let my man think *he* owns *me*.
I must admit, I'm really quite a bitch.

0.1

John Douglas Millar

There I go but for the and the in the swarm and the morass the for the in the blushing morning I go with the for the in the light the grass swaying gently gold in the for there for gun glass there iris there for the in me in is not it swaying grasses with a view across to the in the golden and then the grass the gold somehow light you in the iris shattered the water eye the waterfall in the for the in cold and in cold moss is in the so hand mud there in the rock I did there did not I did in there in that in the slow course of the moon from in the in those were my hands my veins the flame across my hand in the room the moon the slow crossing in the across there in that not I water across the in my out dawn fire too was I in the was it a swallow we go in the on the in the on fire dawn behind the house gable in the and creek and crack in heard through that warm the waterfall and the birch thicket that is whorled in mist bindweed bogwort wild garlic leafmould dung tang scent out the in that with the morning birdsong pine reek gables creek crack like bone the stone of the house cool bluebells in the in gorge of in sunlight goosebumped lilac veins in the swarm of dark exile in time here in the scratched reel of celluloid in the scratched reel of in memory dark in the peat water rainbow tobacco smoke fall cut in the tears the scar now in the with my on the street the territory borrowed tunnel transfiguration of the in the of the in me of the mine of love

Five Poems from:
THE RING CYCLE – *a circus of follies*
Brian Johnstone

Dividing Line

Silence – you insist on it –
takes you by the throat,
forces you to breathe

as each step hangs you
in the balance,
draws you to the line.

From there to here
the wire divides
the air above the ring,

cuts failure from success.
No net is your style,
your small vanity, proof

of something that
your hands stretch out
to touch, grip light

in cruciform, upon the pole.
Out there tomorrow
looms up on the far side

of today. Tomorrow where
they stretch the wire again
and you step into time.

Long Shot

It's primed and ready for the off. Stock rigged,
positioned, checked for glitches, flaws. The angle
of trajectory exact, net tensed and stretched,

the whole shebang all set to launch its prize
right across expectant air. She knows full well
they chose her for her size, her slight build

an advantage they can not afford to do without,
a background in the shows as fitting for the road
as could be hoped. She loves the job, she's not afraid

to own to anyone; loves the ever pregnant pause
before the cannon's shot; loves the rush, the sheer hit
of the act, the heights she never would have gained

left to herself. Bang goes the gun and she's a trace
of smoke, a passing blur that was herself, projectile
in the moment that it takes, as mad for it as ever

as she hits the spot they'd worked out for her
in the prep. Job done, she bounces to her feet
and bowing, snaffles the applause like meat.

A Certain Swing

The climb will rest her mind. Hand over hand,

it takes her closer to the bar. One hundred stares,

the chances that she's open to, all pick her out,
a posed apotheosis stretching for the space,

the air she steps out into, taking with her
nothing but her skill. Her trust is in the game.

It is no game. As serious as love she moves
in arcs, censer at a liturgy. The crowd believes

in miracles; she in time. One on one, they meet,
a moment not too soon. Her hands are there,

his take them, grasp on grasp, hand over hand.

The Caring Blade

Hooded, blind, I'm stood
against a wall. Vile things
that look to happen to me
never do. He slips them in
a millimetre, less, from flesh
that's learned never to flinch,
never to quiver. I feel them,
all the cool blades slip about
my limbs, caress my cheeks
with no more than a rush
of air as they, in series, find
their mark. Then he's blind
too. A gasp as once again
his arm is raised, the knives
propelled and I, their target,
not even once emit a sigh,
a groan. I'm left alone since
he's the one who takes it all:
the cheers, the mad applause,
the whistles, cries and roars
he's due. Me too, I think, but
it is not to be. I slip the hood,
step down and quit the ring.
It's his thing now. He's king.

Pitch

He hangs from a hook on the back of a door,
his trailer empty without him. Top hat
and tail coat, britches and whip, he's all there

though his spirit is off in a bar, by the docks,
by the station, on the far side of town. He's trying
to see out the show, keep enough of himself

in the place that it counts, giving his life
to the road. No-one knows him, he thinks,
this far from the pitch, this far from the boasting,

the crying of acts, the touting of improbabilities
he's the ringmaster of. Put the hat on his head,
the clothes on his back, place the whip

in a gloved right hand. All that he needs
is his voice to sound true. The voice he is seeking
in a bottle, a glass, those rings he's left on the table.

'The Whip Hand', another poem from this cycle, was published in Gutter 5.

'Canned laughter' –
that phrase makes
me smile, makes me
think of walking down
a supermarket aisle
and the baked beans
suddenly chuckling at
you, ribaldry from the
sardines, outrageous
snorting from a catering
size tin of pears.

Chaconne
Linda Henderson

Chaconne

Linda Henderson

She's put the television on.

Ten past three in the morning and she has to put her television on. There's many of us don't sleep through but we don't see the need to put the bloody telly on. Excuse my language.

Radio, yes. I often tune into 'Through the Night', but softly so that the music lulls me back to sleep. How can she look at television pictures at three in the morning? How do you answer the quiz questions? How do you follow who's who in a soap, especially those Australian ones, and how can you laugh? How do you laugh at three in the morning – on your own?

I can't make out what she's watching. It's a blur of noise through the wall. Canned laughter. 'Canned laughter' – that phrase makes me smile, makes me think of walking down a supermarket aisle and the baked beans suddenly chuckling at you, ribaldry from the sardines, outrageous snorting from a catering size tin of pears. It'll be American I expect, the show she's watching. I'm not keen on those. I can't understand a lot of what they say. I prefer something much more gentle or a good detective.

I could bang on the wall but with the sound up that loud she wouldn't hear – Mrs Maceeevor! Mrs Maceeeeevor!! Could you not turn it down a touch?

That's her – Maceeevor. When I first moved in I spotted her name over her doorbell and knocked – I didn't want to make her jump – the doorbells here are worse than a fire alarm. I said 'Mrs MacIvor?' With a long 'I' as in 'aye-aye, Captain' and before I could introduce myself she'd butted in 'It's Maceeeevor'. I said, 'Begging your pardon,' and for a moment we stared at each other and were at a loss as to how to continue. So in the end, when there was no sign she was going to invite me in, I said, 'Lovely morning,' and started to back down her path. She said, 'where are you from?' So I said, 'I'm next door. Your new neighbour.' She laughed a little, false tinkling laugh.

'No, dear. I meant where do your people belong?' She had a posh Perthshire accent. Jenny had already told me my neighbour was from 'Sconn', though I couldn't help myself correcting her, saying surely she meant 'Scone', with a long o as in 'Oh! For the Wings of a Dove'. And we laughed at me being an old school teacher. Mrs MacIvor with an eee was from Scoon and we both knew it.

So I said, 'I'm from Skye.'

'No. I mean where were you born? You're not Scottish.' It was a statement, not a question.

'Am I not?' was all I gave her and retreated round past her pink hydrangea to my own door.

Now it's some singing and applause and another one singing in just the same overwrought way as though they were about to lose everything in their lives. Does nobody sing *sotto voce* these days? It'll be one of those competitions. Have you got what it takes to be a star? Will that make you a better, happier, more generous person? Will you live life to the full, love and be loved? Or is it the money, empty adulation, hunger?

Perhaps I should ring for Jenny but the poor girl needs her rest. I'll have a wee word in the morning. I could put a coat over my nightie and go round – hit her doorbell, she'd hear that. Yes, I could ring her doorbell and run away. In my dreams!

But what if the fright killed her? I couldn't live with that.

So, I'll lie awake and plead, 'Mrs Maceeevor, please Mrs Maceeevor let us have some peace. Please let us sleep, let us sleep.' And the mantra may work.

The next morning I open my door to a bright day and so does Mrs Maceeevor.

'A grand day.' She announces.

'Too bright too early,' I give her back. 'Did you enjoy your TV programmes last night?'

'Oh, I had that Friends thing recorded. I watch them all the way through. All the series. Such nice young people. But they do get up to such a lot we never did and so much money! Are you taking your lunch out today, Mrs Smith?'

She hasn't understood that her Friends kept me awake half the night and annoyed me and made me fret and here I am feeling frazzled and annoyed and she says my name on a rising note ending with a tight 'ith' like a mouse's squeak. I can tell that she thinks that it isn't my real name, that I've made it up, come here, *in cognito*, from a dodgy past or I'm pretending I'm on some adulterous weekend in a seventies sitcom. You didn't have telly through the night in those days and there was no recording, of course. It ended properly with a black screen at midnight. Perhaps one day I'll sidle up to her – sidle as far as my zimmer allows – more like a crabbing action really. I'll crab over to her and whisper, 'It isn't Smith actually. It's Beecham but it's spelled B-e-a-u-c-h-a-m-p, Beauchamp, as in the French. Madame Beauchamp, to you dear.'

But I won't. I married the violinist, Sidney Smith, and in those days you took your husband's name, no question about it. If I'd been on the stage, or been a musician myself, I could have hung onto my own, professionally I suppose – Moss, Muriel Moss. Acquaintances would have introduced me as 'Have you met the pianist, Miss Muriel Moss?' But I was a teacher. It really is a peach of a morning.

So, in 1965 Miss Moss took a group of her schoolchildren to a Saturday morning concert at the local cinema and afterwards, in the throng in the foyer with one of the little darlings gone astray, a kind young man with floppy blond hair, wearing an ordinary brown lounge suit and carrying a violin case asked if he could help in any way. The following summer Miss Moss left school for the holidays and came back in September as Mrs Smith. I can remember writing it up on the blackboard for the children. Of course, the little ones carried on calling me, simply, 'Miss'.

Sidney worked his way through the orchestral desks to become leader of the Royal Philharmonic. He taught a little, directed his own chamber group and would do the odd thing for Radio 3. It was doing the odd thing for Radio 3 that killed him. He was on a train heading for the London studio but it was the one that never got past Clapham Junction. December 1988.

There's a brief knock, a key in the door.

'Only me,' Jenny's cheerful voice, doing her morning round. 'How's tricks, Mrs S? Had a good night?'

I give her a glum upside down grin and point to the dividing wall.

'Bit loud was it?'

'Three in the morning. I could have done without Friends at three in the blasted morning.'

''Spect she couldn't sleep.'

'Asleep in front of it, more like. Oblivious to anyone else. They should make a dead man's handle like they have on the trains. If your hand slips off the remote control the sound cuts. But I'd only mean it to work if she went to sleep – I didn't mean if she died. Though it would of course. Oh dear I am all at sea this morning. It was such a frightful night.'

'I'll see what I can do,' Jenny chuckles. 'How long were you awake?'

'Long enough to do yesterday's Times Crossword. It wasn't a hard one, mind.'

'Are you going to walk round to the lunch today, Mrs S? I think it's mince and tatties, jelly to follow.'

'Mince and tatties. There's a school dinner if ever there was.'

Jenny potters round, washes a cup I've left on the sink, checks the personal alarm is working, looks into the toilet watching for signs I'm becoming unhygienic. She's subtle, is our Jenny. Not one to wag her finger and treat you like a naughty child. She's usually cheerful though there was a spell when I think she'd split up from a boyfriend – or it might even have been a girlfriend. She might be, I think – and we couldn't raise a smile off her. She was in and out with barely a word. Then a week or two later she was her old self, bright and breezy and nothing said about it. I'm not the sort that asks, not one to poke my nose in, but I couldn't help overhearing the chatter at the community lunch. I make myself go over to the lunch club a couple of times a week but I'm not a great one for joining in. I'll take a book and try to get a table to myself. I think if I stop doing this I shall become a recluse and then the powers that be will start to visit and check up on me and disturb me all the more. So I make sure they see enough of me and I dress up a little. It keeps my clothes aired.

'Shall I send the bus round at twelve for you? I'll book you a place.'

'No,' I say. 'Not today, Jenny. I couldn't face school dinners today. I've a soup in the cupboard and some cheese. I'll make do.'

She closes the door and leaves me in blessed peace.

I read a little, then put on my good coat and shoes and walk across the square to the shop in the community building. I don't so much walk as shuffle with the zimmer these days. Funny they built the shop with a door not wide enough to get the frames inside. They remembered a grab handle and a ramp and it's not two or three steps to get to the counter but we all have to park our frames outside like so many shopping trolleys. There's been incidents of stolen frames, or at least the lifting of the wrong one by accident. No one was actually prosecuted. Jenny solved it very calmly with a few bright stickers. I have swans – a black one by my left hand and a white one to the right. 'Tchaikovsky. Swan Lake,' she says, 'Get your pumps on, Mrs S.' But it reminded me of Septembers, first days at school, assigning coat hooks to bewildered faces, best guessing who'd be a jumping dog and who'd like horses and who'd be happy with a frog.

I buy my newspaper and one of those muesli bars that I find such a comfort at about four in the afternoon before Jenny looks in with the hot supper at six. I pass a couple of old men. Well, we're all old here but there is something else I mean by 'old' when it's men. I don't so much as pause with the zimmer, all it takes is a little lift of the left hand, just to be sociable.

Back in the flat I make up a soup and pull something that announces itself as cheese from the fridge. Sidney, I can feel turning in his grave at the thought that we'd have ever served red rubber to guests at our table. We liked good things, food and wine and music and life and love, making love, I mean. Always.

I sit in my chair and fold the paper to the crossword and I must have nodded off.

'Who Wants to be a Millionaire?' Mid-afternoon re-runs! I wake with a jerk, my neck all out of sorts, a dribble of saliva on my chin. No more. I have had enough. Now it will be Wagner. Time for The Dutchman, I think. As loud as I can stand it. Wagner, not my favourite composer but can come in handy at times like this. And suddenly, as I wipe my chin and start to edge up out of my chair, Sidney is there standing across the room, poised. He's in his dinner jacket and dickie-bow, his hair, always long but now receding, silvery, catching the sun from the window. He smiles and waits for me to settle back into my chair before lifting his violin to his shoulder. All is silence. I hold my breath and he plays only to me. He plays Bach to me.

He would play that D minor partita, The Chaconne, to wind down. After a concert he'd be fired up for hours, full of the effort of it, the concentration, with energy still to spend. Bach, he'd always end the evening with Bach. So deep; so personal.

'Beautiful Sidney,' I'd say. 'Come to bed, now.'

And he'd lay down his violin on his desk and follow me upstairs and pour the last of his inspiration into love with me.

It happens sometimes, now – the music I mean. He visits and stays and plays for me. And then I sleep.

Extract from the novel
What We're Looking For

Katy McAulay

Plunge tumble plummet drop accelerate nine metres per second per second and everything hits everything. Blood bone rush spark love thump beat fear breath clutching falling is it possible to be sick while falling is it possible. The sky and the sun and the cold and the ground and the heartbeat hand-grasp hair streaming like a flag. It takes twelve seconds to reach terminal velocity, twelve seconds of limbs that flail, twelve seconds while fingers grasp air that's pointless, air too thin to be of any use. A hammer or a feather, they

I'm thinking about John's fall.

fall the same.

    Is it mass or is it gravity is it mass that creates the fall? Travel 56 metres per second, 125 miles per hour, 200 kilometres in the metric system but who would waste time doing the maths? Who would be

It's been three years.

thinking in terms of hours? Seconds are what matters now. The last string of them accelerate, stretch and snap; they are too much then not enough. The horizon the sky the

I still don't understand it.

***

John fell on the day the Higgs boson was born. I say born, but in fact the current understanding is that the particle has always been there, so I suppose it's more accurate to say that he fell on the day the scientists announced they'd found a way to see it. The God particle. I don't know whose idea it was to call it that – the God particle – but it was a smart move on their part, because despite the fact that barely anyone truly understood what the Higgs boson was for, the story of its discovery was getting a lot of attention in the global media that morning.

    Everyone had gathered in the lecture theatre at the Large Hadron Collider in Geneva for the press conference. Professor Higgs and all of the other scientists who'd worked on the research together were waiting in tense silence for Professor Heuer to take his place behind the lectern and tell the world: they had it. They'd been working on the data for years and the atmosphere was buoyant with expectation.

When the announcement was made, the room exploded. I remember watching the rows of men cheer and slap each other on the back. Some even went so far as to punch the air, despite the fact they were mostly European. I suppose they felt the cameras watching. They must have known they were creating a moment in history. The drinking didn't begin until after all of the media had left, but it went on for a long time; most of the researchers were still celebrating in the final hours of the night when John fell from the roof of the half-constructed physics lab where he worked, landing with lethal force on the empty car park below.

I was at the party in Geneva and John was in Glasgow when he fell, so I didn't see it. I wasn't there, but these days I see it all the time.

Sometimes when I see it, he leaps from the building and sometimes it's more of a stumble. Sometimes I imagine it was a mistake. Occasionally when I picture the scene he's afraid or crying, though other times I'm convinced that he was calm. Only one thing never changes.

He never explains himself. There were no witnesses and John left no clues beyond a drawing of the construction site he fell from and a stream of calculations penned onto the white board in his office. The calculations were mostly gibberish. They were mostly incomplete and half-erased. So I don't know what reasoning my brother applied in order to reach the conclusion that he should end his own life that day, just when everything was going his way.

When someone in your family kills themselves, you can bury it or become an expert. If you become an expert there's a good chance it will bury you.

The experts view graphs plotting others who've also done it, read statistics; they learn the most likely age and other commonalities. Some give interviews, start charities. Some campaign. They spend the rest of their waking lives thinking about suicide.

I didn't want to do that. I'd been brought up to know it did no good to dwell on the popular methods, or to discuss the common triggers: my mother killed herself when she was thirty-six and Dad almost never talked of it. Anyway, those sorry statistics you can find so easily if you have the urge to look weren't applicable in my brother's case. I knew John's life was rosy. True, he was one of the few eminent physicists in the world to have publicly disagreed with Peter Higgs' boson theory before it was proved correct, but the discovery of the particle would have brought a surge of journalists to John's door to seek a soundbite and my brother craved publicity.

On the considerable upside was the research project he was leading, which had been awarded a grant of £4.1 million from the Engineering and Physical Sciences Research Council. There was his photograph recently printed in the *New Scientist*. The half-finished building he fell from was a facility under construction to house his growing research team. And then there was the fact that it seemed to me there wasn't a woman alive who wasn't interested in what she could find under the flamboyant clothes my brother liked to wear. Until he died at the age of forty-eight, I watched him hop seamlessly from relationships with senior faculty members at the universities where he worked, to research students at the same. I'd seen women of all kinds dip their chins to look up at him in a way that was beseeching.

Even Julia had done it. Even my wife. I suppose I should have been angrier about discovering my brother in her office in Geneva the day before he died, especially when John was supposed to be hundreds of miles away at a conference in Boston. Finding the pair of them standing so close and the secret intimacy I'd overheard in Julia's voice before she realised that they had an audience – those things were completely at odds with the fact that my brother and my wife had been rivals for years and openly hostile towards each other since the leaving party.

But I hadn't felt anger over their betrayal. I'd only felt empty. I don't know how else to describe it, except for that in that moment, my life felt like it held so little weight, my actions so little consequence, that I went to a bar and sought proof of my existence in the grasping hands of a woman I barely knew and have never spoken to since.

Now. I loved my brother, don't ever doubt it, but I'm going to be honest here – for the reason I've just mentioned and for many others, I also hated him sometimes. I know I could spend the rest of my life feeling bad about that, but I won't. The things John did and the way he liked to behave, there's no chance he didn't know the power behind being able to bring out both feelings in people, even at the same time, and there are plenty of things he did to me that he knew fine well would hurt. He was relentlessly self-focused. There was the way he was with Julia, the birthdays and anniversaries he forgot, his obsession with arguing the opposite point on more or less every topic of conversation just to prove that he could win, the way he crowed over victories.

I'd like to be able to say that he wasn't always that way, but looking back now, even I can see that all of that, all of the ways he put himself first, they were there from the beginning. For a start, it was his fault I made no friends at high school.

I remember the morning of my first day. I was eating toast. There was an old comic wedged under the leg of the kitchen table at the corner where I was sitting and I remember looking down, half-reading the familiar scene while my mother doled out lunch money. She rummaged in her purse for a last coin and the rummaging went on long enough that I knew she was buying time to think.

'Nervous?' she said at last.

I didn't want her to worry. 'No,' I said.

Mum smiled. Her eyes darted across my face. She nearly rested her hand on my shoulder. Down the hallway, I could hear Dad demanding that John exit the bathroom within 30 seconds or rue the consequences. John was taking his time in there because he didn't like school and so he was doing everything he could to make us late for it. I could hear my father's countdown in fragments around the sound of crunching toast in my ears.

'Fifteen... eleven...'

'It's much bigger,' Mum was saying to me. 'It's bigger than your primary school.'

'...nine... seven...'

'So you won't know everyone,' Mum said.

'I know.'

'...four... two...'

'But John will sit with you at lunch time. So you don't need to worry.'

'I'm not worried,' I said, though in truth, there had been a tightness growing between my shoulder blades during the final weeks of the school holidays that summer, as I had thought about the new horizon that lay ahead.

'All right,' she said at last. 'Promise me you'll look for John.'

'All right,' I said and she snapped her purse closed and sniffled her nose, which had become runny, and pushed her hair out of her face. It needed a wash. Even I could see that.

The school lunch hall smelled of old soup. Food was arranged in mounds on a counter: a watery carrot mountain, damp roast potatoes, pea and sweetcorn mix, something brown in gravy. Each trough was lit by a lamp that radiated yellow heat.

The trays were inexplicably wet but I shuffled through them, holding out hope for a dry one. While I searched, an older boy I didn't know grabbed one of the trays I'd discarded and skipped in front of me in the queue.

'Thanks pubehead,' the boy said.

Another first year pupil with shaggy eyebrows was the next in the line. He made a face that was half amusement, half sympathy. 'It's probably your hair,' he said.

And it was strange because the way the first boy had said pubehead; it hadn't been vicious or threatening. It had been absentmindedly offensive. It was like he'd said it out of habit, like that was really my name.

I shrugged. I was suddenly freshly aware of the tightness between my shoulder blades.

'How come everything's so wet?' the boy with the eyebrows asked. Maybe he was trying to make up for the pubehead thing by seeming interested in my quest for a dry tray.

I shrugged again. I kept my hands busy sifting the trays so that I wouldn't touch my curly hair.

Further along the counter there were bowls of custard, bananas and at the end, cubes of cake topped with chocolate icing. The cakes looked dense and delicious. I paused and did the sums; I didn't have enough lunch money, but if I went without custard for the whole week and saved the change without telling Mum, I'd be able to get one on Friday.

Pleased with my plan, I scooped the tray, paid the lady and approached the seating area. It was busy and constantly moving, like an anthill. I didn't recognise anyone. I circled the area, moving slowly along the aisles between the tables, searching for John's face in the crowd without seeing him. My carrots were leaking water into the gravy, cooling it and turning the brown stuff grey.

'Hello?' The first year from the queue, the one who'd also looked for a dry tray, was eating at a table nearby. He raised his shaggy eyebrows and patted an empty chair beside him – the only one left at his table. 'Want to sit here?' he asked.

I thought that sitting with him would be all right but loyalty to John was beating in my heart. I knew that if I took this offer, there'd be no way for my brother to join us.

'Nah,' I told the boy. 'I'm waiting for my friends.'

When John finally arrived, I saw that he hadn't bothered with a tray. He hadn't bothered with any brown stuff either. I suppose he'd done the sums too and decided that the cakes were the only thing worth the money; he had one in each hand and a bottle of milk in his pocket. I was immediately impressed – it hadn't occurred to me that I could have bypassed eating brown stuff and gone straight for pudding.

'John!' I shouted. 'Johnnyboy!' Sometimes Dad called him that when he was feeling affectionate, although he also used the same name on occasion to indicate that he was very angry with my brother. It was a kind of special occasion name, and one I'd never used, so I don't know why I shouted it out then, other than the obvious reason I was so relieved to see him. I'd been waiting for fifteen minutes, which had felt like at least an hour when for all of that time, the first year with the big eyebrows had been eating nearby, watching me endure the shame of sitting at a table all by myself.

I don't know if my use of a name he wasn't called outside of the house made up John's mind for him in that moment, but although he glanced in my direction for long enough that I knew he'd seen I was sitting alone, there was no warmth or recognition in the look he gave me. His eyes slipped across me like marbles on glass and fastened on a group of older boys who were about to leave the hall.

One of the boys was carrying a football. 'Playing?' my brother said to the boy and then he inserted himself into the centre of the pack and left with them.

Moments later, the first year with the big eyebrows gathered up his now crumb-laden tray and also quit the scene.

'See you later, pubehead,' he said as he passed me by.

That was how I became pubehead – the name that followed me for the next five years of my life – and let's face it: no-one wants to be friends with someone called pubehead. It was also the first time that John publicly betrayed me. I know it seems a minor betrayal now and certainly considering everything that came afterwards, it was, but it's one that still stings.

I suppose that what's especially disappointing is that I should have learned from it. I should have decided there and then not to ever trust that my brother would do anything for me if it involved deviating from the path of his own self-interest.

It's a shame. If only I'd worked that out early, I could have avoided a lot of agony.

The Boys of Summer

Wayne Price

Powell didn't complete his walk up to the church after his mother's cremation, though he'd set out determined to return to it one last time. The ordeal of facing family members he'd hoped never to meet again had left him exhausted after the brief, sterile service; and besides, something obscure inside him rebelled at the thought of actually confronting the once so familiar building – its long low porch and squat, ugly little bell tower – again now. He stopped in a patch of sunlight between trees and meditated on the feeling of resistance that had risen up quite suddenly in him. It wasn't exactly fear, he decided, or perversity. It was a question of doing things in the right order; of not rushing back blindly into the past like some sentimental old fool. Now that the trial of the funeral was over he would take things at his own pace, and clear-sightedly. There was nothing pulling him back; no obligation. He had chosen freely to return, and he would – but tomorrow, maybe. He was in full control.

Still, he was acutely aware of the old place somewhere above him through the woods, just half a mile or so away now after his long, slow wander along the stream, the Sychnant, smaller now than in his boyhood, that drained the forested slopes on either side. In his mind's eye he could see the church very clearly, perched on its steep, tussocky hill, the neglected graves in its burying ground almost tumbling into the springs that fed the little river at his feet. Twelve hundred years since the first burials there. He tasted blood and realized he'd been gnawing at the insides of his lips, a life-long, annoying habit. He sat on a smooth stone at the stream's edge and lit a cigarette.

The sun was warm for March. Across the stream the straight dark pines had given way to a small copse of silver birches, their first leaves just beginning to bud against the pale blue sky. A cold breeze shivered their topmost branches and a moment later he felt it on his bald head and the backs of his hands. The cigarette made him feel even more weary for some reason. He tossed it, half-smoked, into the current and watched it bob downstream. An early hornet hovered as if inquisitively in front of his face, then darted sideways and disappeared. There was no other sign of life, not even birdsong. He rose awkwardly and carried on along the path, deciding to end his walk at the waterfall pool. It couldn't be much further, he knew.

As soon as he arrived at the pool he regretted coming back to it. He remembered swimming waist-deep here as a boy, but now he could have waded to the fall itself and only soaked his ankles. The water spilled thinly and tamely down its small mossy cliff. It was like water being poured carefully from a jug, laving some old man's bearded face. He shook his head, wondering at the change. A wooden walkway had been built along the side of the fall. Even the privacy of the place was gone.

The farmhouse he was staying at, on the hillside above Aberdare, was divided into three holiday lets. Under an assumed name, Powell had rented the loft – a small studio apartment – for the weekend of his return. The evening of his arrival he'd introduced himself to the young English owners, eaten the last of the dry and tasteless sandwiches he'd brought with him on the day-long drive, then lay flat on the bed and fell into a long, dreamless sleep until dawn. Now, this second evening he cooked himself a warm meal of tinned potatoes and tinned chicken before settling into an armchair and working methodically through the local newspaper, cover to cover. As it grew dark he found himself growing restless despite the unaccustomed exercise of his afternoon walk. Tossing the newspaper onto the floor he stood and made his way out onto the balcony overlooking the farmyard. He lit a cigarette and stared down at the scribble of distant streetlights covering the floor and lower sides of the Cynon valley, snaking away between the hills. The dark, forested domes of the mountains loomed bleakly over it all. At wide intervals on the high slopes, single white lights gleamed like stars. The windows of farmhouses much like the one he was staring from, Powell reflected. He didn't suppose anyone was staring distantly back.

A door opened below him and he heard two men light cigarettes and then begin talking softly in the shadow of his balcony. The owners had told him that stone masons were renting the flat below his. They were staying for as long as it took to complete some restorations on a local big house – some coal baron's pile from the 19th century. He hadn't been curious enough to carry on the conversation, and he hadn't liked the fact that the owners were so keen to distribute information. He'd nodded politely and left it at that.

The voices under his feet broke into low laughter and he felt suddenly uncomfortable at hovering so close above them, unnoticed in the dark. He wondered if he should clear his throat, or cough. In the end he simply waited, almost motionless, until they finished smoking and returned indoors.

The next morning was even clearer and brighter than the one before – more like June than late March, Powell reflected, unless you noticed the bare trees, or the sly breeze that every so often lifted unexpectedly and instantly chilled the skin.

He decided to kill most of the morning on the sunny balcony, smoking, and then drive his hired car straight to the church rather than walking along the stream again. There was a small pub opposite the graveyard and if he set out just before noon he knew he could buy lunch there and take a settling drink before looking around.

Driving the narrow road through the woods, he was astonished at the flood of clear, unbidden memories that seemed to rear up at every turn. The sharp corner where, one summer half a century ago, he'd lost control of his bicycle and careened wailing into the pines; the gated footpath into deeper woods he had never explored but often wondered about in his boyhood; the graveled lay-by, now a modern picnic area with benches, where his father had once photographed him holding up like a fisherman's catch the perfect, still-warm body of a barn owl that had lain freshly killed at the side of the road. Where would they have been heading to then, in the old Morris Minor? Over the mountain to the next valley, he supposed. Maybe to some strained family gathering in Ferndale or Merthyr. And they'd been late. Yes – he remembered now – his mother shouting out of the car window as his father arranged the heavy dead bird, wings spread wide in his skinny arms: what are you doing with that dead thing? We're *late*, Bill. Take it from him. Take it from him! What are you making him *do*?

He braked sharply. Two men, youths, plastic carrier bags in their hands, had emerged suddenly from the trees and in his daydream he'd almost clipped the nearest. They both flinched back onto the grassy verge and as he accelerated away Powell watched them staring after him in his rearview mirror.

The pub was opening as he arrived. A young girl was propping the door wide with an antique flat-iron and she straightened up to let him pass.

Be with you now jest, she said cheerfully. I'm letting a bit of sun in.

He went through to the bar, took a menu from one of the tables and studied it.

Soon the girl appeared, smiling brightly. Now then, she said.

A pint of Bass, please, he said. And the ham and eggs.

Food will be a bit longer, she apologized. Chef's jest arriving now.

He nodded. And it's okay to eat outside?

Oh yes! I'll bring it out when it's ready. A treat to be able to, isn't it?

An older woman looked in to the bar from what seemed to be the kitchen. She nodded at Powell and disappeared again.

The girl topped up the head of the pint and handed the brimming glass to him. I don't think I've seen you here before. Jest visiting is it?

That's right, he said.

You should take a look at the church. It's very old. Over a thousand years, bits of it.

I might do that.

You can't go inside, mind. It's only open once a month nowadays. Vandals, see. Though what they come all the way out here for I don't know.

Oh, he said, and smiled. She began sorting cutlery into sets, wrapping each bundle of knife, fork and spoon in a green paper napkin. There are some very old poems about this place, in fact, he said on a sudden impulse. Then, embarrassed and not knowing how else to answer her stare, he recited in his pulpit voice:

> *Aberdare, Llanwynno through,*
> *All Merthyr to Llanfabon,*
> *A more terrible thing there never was*
> *Than the cutting of Glyn Cynon.*

Well, she said, after an awkward pause. There's nice, isn't it?

It's very old, he added lamely. It's translated from the Welsh, of course.

I s'pose it would be, she said.

Actually, I used to be the parish priest here, he blurted. He felt a blush beginning at the base of his throat and a flicker of panic in his stomach, but felt compelled to go on.

Is that right? she said, looking up.

He nodded. I was christened here, married here, and ordained here. But I won't be buried here, he added, again surprising himself with his frankness.

She narrowed her eyes, though the smile stayed on her lips. So you're retired now then?

Oh, yes, he lied, smiling back at her reassuringly. But anyway, parish priests get moved around all the time, you see. I left here before you were born, probably.

To be honest with you, I never knew priests did retire, she said, taking up another clutch of cutlery from a tray under the bar. I thought they just went on forever, like that Father Jack on the telly. She laughed at her own joke and Powell smiled again.

Well, that's the Catholic Church, he said. It's a bit different in the Church in Wales.

I'm not religious at all in any kind of churchy way, she confided. My nan was, like, but that was chapel. But it's a comfort isn't it? It's always there for you, I mean. It's not like we're just animals, is it?

He shook his head. I suppose not, he said. He took a careful sip at his beer.

She laughed suddenly. Look at me talking all philosophical now when I've got work to do. She slipped away to the kitchen. I'll get your food ordered, she called back as she left.

He carried his drink outside to the sunshine, wondering at himself. Foolish, he thought, utterly foolish, but instead of regret or fear he felt only a dim sense of satisfaction and relief. He took a deep breath and settled himself at one of the bench tables. It gave him a clear view of the church porch. There it was, both familiar and strange somehow, just across the road from him. He'd never really expected to come back; had never expected to find the courage; but here he was.

The table was in exactly the spot he remembered from childhood. How many generations of wooden tables had rotted away and been replaced between then and now? he wondered idly. They would cycle here on hot summer days in the long holidays – Lefty, Shepherd, Hopkins and himself – and look for the dregs left behind by lunchtime drinkers. Sometimes they'd have to fish wasps out of the deep pint glasses with twigs. He grinned at the memory of it. The intense joy they took from tasting the sour, flat dregs of King's Ale or Whitbread Bitter, just because it was found, and free, and they'd cycled long, thirsty miles for the chance of it, and because they were boys in summer and the dark stale taste was the exact taste of adulthood, and all the knowledge and liberties it promised.

Crunching over gravel, a silver hatchback drew in to park beside his own car. Two children, a boy and a girl, spilled out ahead of a man and woman who followed some way behind them up to the pub. The kids, dressed almost identically in jeans and blue hooded sweatshirts, lingered in the doorway, jostling each other and giggling. The mother, arriving, ushered them in and rolled her eyes at Powell. The father ignored him.

The initial lightness Powell had felt after speaking to the bargirl was fading and in its place a vague feeling of impatience was growing. He was beginning to regret ordering food. Better to have made his peace and then moved on at once, maybe. What was he gaining now by drawing the whole thing out?

High, wispy clouds had dimmed the early afternoon by the time his meal appeared. The older woman brought it out to him and made no attempt at conversation. He ate quickly, shivering a little each time the hilltop breeze circled to his patch of weakening sunlight.

A powerful, charcoal grey Audi drew up directly in front of the entrance, the features of the man driving it shadowy behind the long, low glass of the windscreen. Powell mopped up the last of his egg yolk with a cold tile of ham, paying the car no obvious attention but aware all the time that the driver had remained sitting there behind thick, slanted glass, facing him, the smooth, quiet engine still purring. Finally, Powell pushed his plate away and looked up. Yes – the driver was definitely watching him. Defiantly, Powell drained off the last of his bitter. But who was he? Please God not a journalist. No, not in that car. An old church acquaintance, maybe? A forgotten face from one of his congregations? Or just some bored businessman, thinking about his pension, not even realizing he was staring? God knows, Powell himself did that often enough.

Finally, the stranger stirred behind the windscreen and the car reversed, smoothly, turned and glided away towards the mountain top and the sprawling valleys towns beyond. Unnerved, Powell lit a cigarette and hardly noticed when the young waitress collected his plate until she said: are you going to take a look at your old church, then?

He forced a tight smile and nodded, but didn't trust himself to speak. He paid for the meal there and then, tipping generously, and stood as she left the table. He could hear his breath entering and leaving his mouth. He stubbed out his cigarette and crossed the road to the iron wicket-gate in the churchyard wall.

For a while he simply sat on one of the neat Victorian graves, away from the shade of the building and the bulky churchyard yews, waiting for his thoughts and emotions to settle. It was a grave he remembered even from childhood because it held the bones of a certain William Powell, Ynysybwl, and when he was a boy, standing on the soft mound, the simple coincidence of seeing his father's name there always sent a faint electric thrill into the soles of his feet. When he felt the cold seeping up through his trousers from the stone he rose to his feet and decided to walk once around the church before leaving. He wasn't completely calm yet, but the few thin clouds at noon had spread into a watery emulsion across the sky and the air was cooling more rapidly now. There was no sense in staying much longer.

On the far side of the church, hidden from the road and pub, the graves were older and in a much poorer state. Many of the box-tombs had long ago collapsed inwards or outwards and he recalled as a boy climbing into them, looking for bones and wedding rings. All the headstones listed drunkenly towards the marshy bottom of the slope. Century by century the ground was slipping. A smell of rotting vegetation drifted up from the fringe of pines that marked the lower edge of the cemetery some fifty yards below.

It was only as he climbed back level with the church that he noticed the two youths and recognized them from the near miss in his car. They were sitting on a dilapidated wooden bench, their backs to the graveyard wall. The plastic bags they'd been carrying were empty now and a small army of cider cans, some upright, some folded and toppled on their backs, littered the ground at their feet. Powell halted instinctively but realized he would have to go on climbing towards them or lose face. They watched him impassively to begin with, then the taller of them, still wearing only a vest and white baseball cap above his jeans despite the new chill in the air, stood and stooped and wiped his palms on the long skinny posts of his thighs. The one left seated grunted in reply as Powell nodded and said, fine afternoon, lads. Have you walked far?

The question seemed to take the youth by surprise. He thought for a moment, staring up from his seat as if dazed. From over Miskin way, he said at last, evasively.

The punch from the taller man was clumsy but it came from behind, surprising Powell, and he fell forward more from shock than the actual weight of it. But by then they were on him anyway, their bony knees dropping onto his spine and kidneys, fists hammering at the back of his neck and head. He felt a clawing at his throat and underneath him at his waist and thought they were about to throttle him, or worse, and his long animal moan of fear seemed to infuriate them even more. They took hold of his hair and ground his face into the cold grass and dirt. Then they wrenched his arms back and he realized they'd been removing his tie and belt to truss him. Though winded, he bucked and squirmed desperately against this new helplessness, but it was no use. They were drunk and slow but he was utterly overpowered now. He knew, with the detached, calm clarity of despair, that any hope of resistance had been beaten from his body.

Without rolling him from his stomach they found his wallet, mobile phone and car keys. He wondered suddenly if they would torture him in some way for the codes to his credit cards, but they were too drunk or too hurried to think of it. He heard grass being torn up by its roots at the side of his head and the noise was oddly magnified, like country sounds at night, and then they were forcing handfuls of it – damp grasses, grainy soil and the spear-tips of mangled rushes – between his teeth to silence him. When he clenched his jaws they smothered his nose so roughly his eyes teared and as soon as he gasped to breathe his mouth was crammed again with another springy, sickening mess of roots and stems. He stopped resisting then. He knew that if he gagged at the sharp points of rushes pricking the roof of his mouth he would drown on his vomit. With a final effort of will he turned what remained of his strength inwards, waiting simply for his attackers to finish with him and make their escape.

He didn't know how long they'd been gone before he allowed himself to move again, but the sun had dipped below the hills and when he rolled onto his back and strained to sit upright he realized he was shivering violently. A car rumbled by on the other side of the wall. There must have been other cars too, he thought, maybe people walking even, but he hadn't been aware of them. Patiently, still concentrating hard on resisting his nausea, he began forcing the rough bolus out of his mouth, levering it with the root of his tongue. Only when his mouth was almost empty did he allow himself to turn his head and throw up onto the grass at his side. He spat to clear the bile from his lips, then rested again before working on his tied wrists. The knot had been rushed and it soon loosened enough to let him slip one hand free. He unwound the belt from his ankles then and pulled himself trembling onto the wooden bench. He knew his hire car would be gone: he'd heard them gloating when they found the keys. Well. He had no intention of reporting any of it yet. It was unthinkable that the local police or press should connect his name to this place. He would get to Cardiff somehow, the next day, and report the car and wallet stolen from there. There'd be nothing newsworthy about that. Not in the city.

When he felt he could trust himself to walk again he stood, straightened his jacket and made for the cemetery gate. Above all, he mustn't be seen yet. Anyone seeing him now, before he'd had time to clean himself up and recover his wits, might call the police whatever he said. The waterfall came to mind. He could wash himself there, then make his way back to the road along the river path. There was enough daylight left.

Looking down into the swirling surface of the waterfall pool, it occurred to Powell that for most of his adult life he would have felt the need to pray in circumstances like this, and now nothing could seem more bizarre. Instead, he found himself reflecting on the way he had gone about sealing off each period of his life from the one before, always irrevocably. His turning to God in his twenties had brought with it a quiet but absolute break from all the intense, unhappy loyalties and disappointments of his adolescence. And then his disgrace, twenty one respectable years later; had that been just another instinctive way of sealing off a worn-out past, of making any return impossible? And why? Surely other people lived differently? Why had this been the shape of *his* life – no pattern or continuity or grace, just an ugly series of secrets, concealments, and ever widening spaces? The middle years of his life, for God's sake, when so many people grew into some kind of knowledge of themselves, might just as well have been lived by a stranger inside his skin.

He sat heavily on a tree stump, knowing suddenly that if he didn't sit at once his legs would give way. With every breath a deep needle was rising and falling in his chest, rhythmically, like the tooth of a slowly turned sewing machine. His arms hung like iron from his shoulders and his breathing whistled in his nostrils where blood had crusted inside. He was sixty seven now. Whatever the reasons, he had failed to make any sense of life in the way he had lived it. That was the pitiful truth of it, he supposed. And maybe it wasn't so strange. For all he knew, anyone might feel this way if they opened their eyes to see. Those two thugs, for a start: Christ, what pattern could they have in their lives? And why should he expect his life to have any more meaning than theirs? What kind of vanity was that? Theology, philosophy, poetry, morality: all just ways of treading on water, walking on language instead of the hard dirt we would have to come back to in the end. He tasted the grass roots and marshy soil on his tongue again and tried to spit but was too dry. He wanted to smoke now, desperately, but of course they'd taken his cigarettes and lighter. If he had the power, he thought, he would kill them now, just for that and nothing else.

There were owl pellets at his feet, he noticed – three of them, quite fresh, smooth as wrens' eggs. With an effort he bent forward and gathered them up. The largest of them he crumbled on his open palm, separating out the tiny white bones of voles and mice. One fragment looked like a horse's jaw-bone in miniature. He thought of the great barn owl he had held spread-eagled like a trophy, or an offering, for his father's camera. Where was that photograph now? As soon as his mother died he had paid for his parents' narrow terraced house to be cleared without his interference. Had that been done yet? Maybe the picture was still in its album somewhere, in a box or a cupboard or a cluttered bedroom drawer. Well – it was too late anyway. He didn't have the courage to change the arrangements now and deal with the house himself, all the past still crouching in its low rooms, and all around it the shadows of old neighbours stirring behind net curtains.

When the police had come to the Manse, at dawn, another lifetime ago now, his first feeling was of relief that the dream-like, sudden unravelling of his life wasn't happening at his parents' house, in that little terraced trap of faces and gossip. He groaned to himself at the memory, almost overcome with a welling up of confusion and shame. The stabbing in his chest was quickening. *A more terrible thing*, he recited to himself deliberately, as if to slow it again, *a more terrible thing there never was than the cutting of Glyn Cynon*. Then anger rolled through him, though he couldn't have said if it was fury at himself or at the face of a world which had never, in all his sixty-seven years, altered its blank, unmeaning expression for him. He moaned aloud, feeling tears of pain and self-pity welling to his eyes against his will, and slapped his palms clean. At a faint sound in the undergrowth he looked up and saw a fox, its coat a dark, smoldering red, making its way swiftly through the ranks of trees. Completely unaware of him it moved in strange, stiff-legged bounds, springing as if for pleasure on the pine-straws' soft bed. From somewhere out of sight on the streamside path below, voices were drifting to him. He struggled to his feet and felt the needle stitching in his heart again, deep down in the muscle beneath the bone. He steadied himself, then began the slow walk toward them.

Mezzanine

Vicki Jarrett

From the top of the racking, if you tilt your head and let your eyes go slack, you can see right through the perforated steel of the mezzanine floor, down to Groceries below. Then further, if you stay with it, through that floor to White Goods on the ground level. Must be, what? Sixty foot, give or take.

It's a rush, especially when I'm leaning out and holding on by only one or two fingers (the best way). That jolt of vertigo when the total height snaps into focus, the feeling there's only a few twigs of bone and stringy loops of muscle keeping me anchored to the living world. It's fucking terrifying. Makes me dizzy and weak but I do it every time. Because I can. Because I can feel all that and not lose it, not shake or cry or scream. I am in control.

There's that.

Then there's the feeling that comes next. Like I'm balanced, almost weightless, right at the very top of an idea so simple and perfect that it'll clear away all the shit in my head and make everything line up and fit together properly. That tipping point where all the effort of getting up there is over and the reward will be total lasting peace. Exactly there. That pinnacle of glorious anticipation before I go tearing down the other side, hair streaming, wind in my face, headlong into another brick wall. Not the Answer after all. Just another dud. I smash into but not through it. And I have to start again.

Can't

hang around here forever though. Work to be done.

Aisle 12. Kitchenware. Check my folder. Vyleda mop heads – 3; mop handles – 2; Hozzlehock pegs – 2 standard size plain, 1 multi-coloured, 2 jumbo pegs with the springs. Section 7. Shelf 10. I don't know who racks the stock in the warehouse when it arrives but it's as if they deliberately put the difficult to carry stuff right at the top. Mop handles being a case in point. The heads I can safely drop from any height and they'll be fine but the handles are different. Bits can get broken off. I have to find a way of carrying them down without losing my grip.

I leave the folder and clamber sideways, hand over hand, gripping the metal struts, pushing my toes between cardboard boxes for a foothold. We're not supposed to do it like this. Health and Safety and all that crap. But there are only so many ladders and so many stands and never enough to go around. If you always try to do things by the rules then you'll never get anything done at all.

My guidance teacher at school used to say if I didn't improve my attendance record and study for my exams then I'd 'end up stacking shelves at the supermarket.' Like that was the very worst thing that could happen to a person. Mr Smiley was surprisingly stupid. I remember I used to think teachers had to be clever, but the longer I stayed in school the more I noticed that most of them didn't have a scooby, and some weren't even half-way bright. That was a real

let down.

As it turned out,

I don't stack shelves. (Fuck you very much, Mr Smiley.) I'm behind the scenes, supplying those that do. I'm what's called a Picker. I write down what's missing from the shelves in a special folder full of plastic-covered shelf plans, using a special pen so it can be wiped clean at the end of each shift, then I go to the warehouse and load everything needed into tall metal trolleys and send them down in the lift to the shop floor. The shelf-stackers take it from there. I wonder whether Smiley would consider what I do better or worse than shelf-stacking. I wonder why I wonder that, because I honestly couldn't give a fuck.

I work from seven in the evening till midnight. The twilight shift, they call it. Makes it sound romantic and maybe a bit mystical, like we're a bunch of fucking elves or pixies or something, tippy-toeing around the store in the half light, sprinkling fairy dust and working our magic to make sure everything's perfect for the humans by morning. Hope I'm not bursting your bubble here but it's really not like that. No magic. No pixies. Just shit work and minimum wage. Same old same old.

Mum used to say 'don't pick it, it'll only get worse.' The phrase registers in my head every single time I clock on, like it's programmed into the card puncher. Card in, ka-chunk, fucking annoying advice out. It's irritating the way her nonsense hangs around, wormed into unexpected places, wherever there's a gap. It's like she's haunting me before she's even

properly

dead.

I stop for a little light refreshment. Section 5. Shelf 8. Still there. In a dusty old box of cracked draining racks that someone should really throw out, a half bottle of Bell's, tucked down the side. The very thing. Onwards. I take a wide swing out, one arm gripping, the other swooping in an arc. As a species, we should've stayed in the trees. There's something about climbing like this. Feels somehow satisfying. Real.

Mum also used to say 'little pickers wear bigger knickers.' Never mind big knickers, I'm wearing cycle shorts under my blue polyester uniform skirt. All the female pickers learn that on their first shift. When you're high in the warehouse racking, even if you use the ladders like you're supposed to, there'll always be some smartarse down below ready to pass comment. Be easier if we could wear trousers, but that's against the rules too. Not a big fan of the rules, me.

Right on cue, I get a drawn-out, sarcastic wolf whistle from Davey, pushing a trolley below where I'm pulling packets of pegs out of a box. He hasn't stopped, or even looked up properly, it's just a reflex.

'Away and piss off!' I shout down. Doesn't cost anything to be polite.

'Love you too, Babe,' he calls back over his shoulder, still pushing his trolley towards the lifts.

'Jackie,' I call after him. 'My *name* is Jackie.'

Davey's alright. Some of the others aren't, which makes Davey a Good Guy. The clunk and rattle of his trolley wheels dwindle away to nothing, lost in a few turns of the high sided cardboard maze.

I drop the three mop heads, one after another and they land with muffled thuds. The wooden pegs can be safely dropped as well but not the plastic ones, they're liable to break. I start wrestling the mop handles out of their box. At least there's only two. Heads wear out quicker than handles. Shame people don't have replacement heads for when the ones we've started out with get knackered or worn out. Folk could have a collection of spare heads for different occasions. A head for every day of the week. Useful for those difficult mornings too. Which might not be quite so difficult if I stopped drinking so much. But the thing about drinking,

proper drinking,

till I'm almost-passing-out (but not), is that I get close to the edge,

which is the only place I can feel

alive.

No matter how smashed I get, no matter how physically incapable, there's always part of me sitting in a corner of my head, calmly watching, absolutely sober. Nothing can touch that part of me. Nothing. It's cold. Immune to everything (I've checked it all). I like to get close to it so I can remind myself it's still there. I'm still there. Standing near

the edge

is the only place I can get a grip, feel the shape of things, feel my hold on them.

I wedge the two mop handles under my arm and start climbing down, pausing at each shelf to move the packets of plastic pegs down as I go. It's tricky. My arms are getting tired and the mop handles keep catching on the racking and threatening to lever me off into thin air. But I've done this before. I can handle it.

It's always better to visit the edge deliberately than to wait for it to come and find me. Often, it arrives without warning. I wake up and it's right at the side of my bed and just putting my feet on the floor is taking a step off a cliff, off the edge of the world into the howling black void of space, and I've no idea when or

if

my feet might land again on solid ground.

Made it. I stack everything together on my trolley and take a moment to roll my shoulders, stretch my arms out, imagine them growing and spreading out and out and up and up.

And sometimes the edge stalks me all day, lurking under kerbs waiting to snatch at my ankles when I cross the road, or in the lift shaft where the lift should be but hardly ever is, waiting to suck me down. Or in the silences I don't know how to fill when people talk to me.

Wherever there's a

gap.
It could be
anywhere.

My mother came out through the gaps between her father's words and what his silences admitted. I met him, that once, though she didn't want me to. 'There's nothing to be gained,' she said. Another of her stock of ready-made phrases. Her speech was always weighted with them. She hardly ever put words together herself. Her talk was all verbal chicken nuggets – bland, bite-sized and pre-processed. Now she's even lost the ability to choose the right one for the occasion. She'll sit there and smile vaguely, her eyes drowning in themselves, and say things like 'you'll catch your death' and 'what a wicked web we weave...' then trail off and start humming some never-ending tuneless tune.

Lately she doesn't seem to care who I might be but sometimes she hazards a few guesses. Some of the names she comes out with – I'm sure she's never even met folk with those names, she's just pulling them out of the air, or maybe from memories of TV soaps.

Mary? Trisha? Amelia? Gracie?

'Jackie,' I tell her. 'My *name* is Jackie.'

She looks at me and frowns like she's searching through the clutter in her head and I think maybe she's going to find me in there somewhere, but she just shakes her head and says 'A little knowledge is a dangerous thing.'

Finding him was easier than I'd imagined it could be. He wasn't even bothering to hide. As if he had nothing to be ashamed of.

I went to the pub first, steadied myself, then went and sat in his piss-smelling front room and watched as everything I didn't know but half-suspected about my mother's childhood came hissing like steam out through his words and solidified into the shape of a girl struggling to disappear. He gave me a battered box-file of papers, old photos and letters. Said he had no use for them anymore and I may as well take them away. Pandora doesn't know the half of it. Inside that box were packed the overlaid shadows of those who came before him, like a concentrated thunderhead of cause and effect. All the generations coiling up out of it until they clenched together and telescoped

back down,
like the funnel of a tornado, to
me

on the mezzanine floor. I start climbing again. I feel better up high and I left the stock folder up there anyway.

There are holes in everything. Holes, in fact, if you want to take it all the way (and why wouldn't you?), are what the world and everything in it is made of. I've been thinking about this. Atoms, right? They're mostly empty. Electrons and whatever else, whizzing around a big load of nothing. So, the truth of it is, there's more nothing than anything else.

There are more gaps than not-gaps, more holes than

Mum still likes to crochet. She's rotten at it but never lets that stop her. She makes squares with different patterns in endlessly ugly colour combinations then sews them together to make scarves and tea cosies and cot blankets. The results were always misshapen and full of holes but they've got a lot worse recently. Holes are what they're made of now, loosely strung together with wool.

There were similarities. Of course. You can't get away from genetics. It's inheritance. Passed down, hand to hand, one to the next. He was old, but still managing to live on his own. He looked at me as I was leaving, sniffed the whisky on my breath and said, 'the apple never falls far from the tree.'

And what a tree it is. Our family tree. Maybe every family is the same if you peel back the bark and inspect the worm holes. Maybe we all come from the same long line of broken minds, drunks and bastards.

It's like some kind of optical illusion, seeing all the stories layered on top of each other, snapping in and out of focus. Like there's a hidden meaning in the way the pattern shifts, some knowledge to be decoded from the frequency and angle at which new patterns emerge.

I climb

back to Section 5, shelf 8 and the bottle's near enough empty now. Might as well finish it off. The racking lurches to the side as I stash the empty bottle back in the box but I don't let it faze me. The effects of that joint I smoked in the car park are joining forces with the whisky now, setting the outer edges of my perception spinning like a wobbly carousel. I look down and watch the racking twisting round on itself, groaning under the strain into a double helix of contorted metal. Not even going to try and get down that.

I go sideways again, find that narrow gap at the very top of Section 9 and crawl in, shoulders brushing against the boxes on either side. Just a short break and I'll get back to work. It's not bad here. Quite cosy. I could have a nap. No one would notice.

I can feel that the sober part of me that's been observing, taking notes, agrees. Sleep would be a Good Thing. In my dreams,

I'm always
climbing.

A Jewelled Whip

Kevin Henderson

Not to meet yours, Scotland feeling you, not to meet your
acid blue lips;
night in every glass and steel supermarket *extra*,
the breath of dual-carriageway in every aisle, your bliss
not to be found in one of them;
newly cut verges,
French quean, *favour*, great public event... no,
just pure-mental display
defining a brutal destiny.

Hrabal in Dumbarton

Gregor Addison

Hrabal in Dumbarton and Ballantyne's
a cinnamon brick amongst the drab
unasked-for grey, a half-drunk figure
facing eternity and death. How like the town
he drives through? How distant now
from the poet who arrived hot-foot from Ireland,
a price upon his head, asking only patronage
for a special gift. The university
has laid on a fancy party and the Czech
will cut his cake, will answer questions.
But back home, he will write
out of the tumble-down scatter of his memory
and daub the town with brush-strokes all his own.
And so we paint. And so we paint.
Each stroke over the last.

Don't Put One Egg In All Your Baskets

John McGlade

On Friday I went to the Mosque
On Saturday, Synagogue
On Sunday, Holy Mass
On Monday a Calvinist bash
On Tuesday I didn't eat
Being a Buddhist on retreat
So I sated Wednesday's hunger
In the Gurdwara, at langar
(Though not before with candour
I'd rung the bell at the local Mandir)
I had options on day seven
But on Thursday I went to Heaven
Which God said I can't enter
On the grounds: 'No Moral Centre!'

After a reading the collected poems of *ASJ Tessimond*

Steve Harvey

(For Frank Keetley)

I bet the money spent went less amiss
On strippers, nightclub hostesses, and such,
Than sessions of psychoanalysis
That probed and diagnosed but did not touch.

Alone in a Room with God

Mark Russell

Here's a thing about Scotland:
it has only one cold.
Last week my daughter had it.
She said she got it from our one
and only teacher. Several years ago
a Nationalist came to my door:
at that point in history he had it,
and was clearly burdened by it,
but it didn't stop him asking me
to vote for him. Before I could
answer he sneezed green globules
in a neat row on my sleeve.
I tried to tell him that I believed
nationalism and religion were the twin pillars
of genocide but he had a bus to catch.
Today I heard on Radio 4
that there was only one taxpayer;
that he was me, and he was you,
that he was everywhere and nowhere,
but that nobody had ever seen him
alone in a room with God.
Should the latter exist, surely he must be
more sociable than that, he who seems
to have multiple personalities
but fittingly, no definite article,
and therefore though he may be
God the Taxpayer among his many
disguises, he is certainly not Scottish.

Fish Tales of a New Pilgrim

Stephen Nelson

The pilgrim's cave,
full of fish!

Sleep
Wet

or

don't
sleep

*

A walk to the shore.
More salt in the wind.

fish
hook
eye

bleeding salt

*

Coastline nets
the land.

Even seagull's wings
won't save you!

*

Born
from salt water,

more salt
in his beard
than a boy
has any
right to.

*

This pilgrim has zeal.

He only has to sneeze
& the herring shoal shivers.

*

God speaks
through gulls
and empty
chip pokes.

Not long now! says the pilgrim,
coughing up the breeze.

*

He waits in a boat,
refusing smokes and alcohol.

Only blind fish
succumb to temptation.

Only hungry pilgrims
eat their fish tails raw.

Digital trees

Colin Will

The dark bark of cherries
is the negative of silver birch,
the same frayed paper,
shiny skin, but light and shade
reversed.

Across the trunk short tracks,
stuttered pits, the information holes
of pianola rolls, Jacquard looms,
Hollerith cards, the negative
of music box pins, a program
for the tree's symphony of sighs,
whispers, whipcracks, broken twigs,
woodwind notes.

The Sentence

Wendy Miller

Och you know
it was like
one of those sentences
that's hard to read
you've to squint your eyes to see it absurd
blur of words on white laptop landscape
odd unsettling somehow insatiable
A head fuck
with no respect
for punctuation
then one day
marching bare-foot into your city
I ran into you in the street
knelt down before you
placed a full stop at your feet

In praise of the city

James Irvine

In the forest I am a tree,
on the beach a grain of sand
In the ocean I am a wave
In the sky I am a cloud
In the city I am human

William Carlos Williams:
First Lines, Found

Kate Tough

The following poems were constructed from sets of lines found very close to each other in the index of WCW's collected works.

The titles are the poet's.

Maggie
with big breasts / under a blue sweater
With sharp lights winking
With the boys busy

Capitalism
The pure products of America
The rat sits up and works his

Maggie Maggie
This, with a face
This woman! how shall I describe her
This woman with a dead face

Creative Scotland Professional Development Application
New books of poetry will be written
Nine truckloads of jewels

Maggie Maggie Maggie
The refrain is grown silent
The revolution / is accomplished

Like Hagar

Olive M Ritch

she is loved,
unloved –

his tone of hands,
warm, cold –

cast out with child –
wanted, unwanted –

in the wilderness –
despair, hope –

our sister's story –
past – present – future

Scotland's War Song

James Irvine

A treasury of men are we
and no great mischief if we fall
It's England expects our duty
to die in greater numbers so
There'll always be an England sung

Exile and Immigration

The Mouse Deer Kingdom
Chiew-Siah Tei

Picador, RRP £8.99, 374pp

Chiew-Siah Tei's first novel, *Little Hut of Leaping Fishes,* followed the rise of Chai Mingzhi from small boy to learned Mandarin during the later Qing period (late 19th Century). The book climaxes when the Boxer Rebellion forces Chai, his sister, his niece and the Englishman Martin Gray, to flee China for the land yet to become Malaysia. *The Mouse Deer Kingdom* continues Chai's story, but is less a sequel than a stand-alone novel featuring many of the same characters. Tei manages to bring in new readers while avoiding a 'previously on...' moment, so unfamiliarity with *Little Hut* is no handicap.

The focus of the narrative is now Engi, an indigenous boy taken in by Chai. Arriving together, it is inevitable the group will dissolve through death, departure and betrayal. Pivoting on Engi, the narration flows around other key characters, allowing the reader access to the intricate weave of secrets and lies as it begins to fray. In turn each bond of loyalty is broken leaving Chai, with Engi watching from the wings, alone. This narrative arc has an inbuilt frustration for the reader. As characters break from their orbit around Chai they disappear, leaving a number of loose ends and untold stories. The fates of Martin, and Chai's niece, Jiaxi, in particular are unsatisfactorily concluded.

Tei, like fellow Malaysian Tan Twan Eng, is at her best when describing Malaysia. Gentle, poetic descriptions of the landscape and deft, almost Dickensian pen-portraits of the hardships faced by both displaced natives and disillusioned incomers are shot through with an obvious deep love for her home country. Malaysia has a long and complicated relationship with migration and colonisation, being at one time or another under the control of the Portuguese, Dutch, English and Japanese and having an ethnically diverse population. As such it is an ideal setting for an exploration of divisions and unity.

At heart it is a novel about exile and immigration, and Tei is excellent on the racial and cultural tensions between natives, incomers, and different immigrant groups. The centring of Engi by a simple switch from third to first person sets up a dynamic dialectic. Initially he is the voice of the forest-dwelling natives whose lives and culture are systematically destroyed by encroaching rubber plantations and the kidnapping of women to become 'wives'. The hopes and fears of the immigrants, educated and not, young and old, Chinese and English, compete for supremacy. This narrative arrangement works to highlight the social and historical forces pulling in diverse directions; the battlefield of indigenous and immigrant populations to this day. As an exploration of these themes, *The Mouse Deer Kingdom* is both sympathetic and honest.

While the majority of historical fiction focuses on one particular event or figure, Tei does something much more interesting. She shows, through the journeys of her characters, the already interconnected nature of the world more than a century ago, and how the movement of people to, from, and around the Far East has both driven and hindered social cohesion. Globalisation is nothing new. In an era when immigration is never out of the news, Tei's book is a timely reminder of both the problems and undoubted benefits the continual movement of people brings. It is infused with the message that more empathy is needed from both sides of the debate, as is an understanding that finding somewhere safe and secure to call home is one of the most basic human instincts. The enduring image from *The Mouse Deer Kingdom* is Chai Mingzhi's signboard, *Chai Family* painted in Chinese Mandarin and English, trampled in the dirt.

— *Totoro*

Thousand-yard Stare

Call of the Undertow
Linda Cracknell

Freight Books, RRP £8.99, 256pp

The myth of the Selkie-folk runs through Linda Cracknell's *Call of the Undertow*, drawing the reader into speculation about how much of cartographer Maggie Thame's new life in Caithness is otherworldly. Yet, this nod to the supernatural is balanced by a pragmatism from both protagonist and author that sees the image of the Selkie superseded by a vivid description of a seal shot through the neck to protect fishing stocks. The myth becomes a metaphor for people "who feel pulled between two worlds", with the realism of the murdered seal containing a note of danger that persists throughout.

Maggie has moved to this isolated community to escape to the "white spaces on the map" and this retreat into the rural is artfully portrayed. Indeed, there is a tone reminiscent of writers such as Kathleen Jamie and Robert MacFarlane in the way that nature is evoked. Observation of the birds of the far North of Scotland punctuates the prose, with Guillemots gathering on the cliff-face as if at "the most raucous Elizabethan playhouse echoing with catcalls and laughter". There is also a playfulness to the explanations of the nicknames given to the various local species, marking the birds as an intrinsic part of daily life. Yet, as with the community itself, Maggie finds that the birds are not so welcoming when they perceive a threat from the newcomer; a Hitchcockian allusion that builds the suspense.

The plot centres around a local schoolboy, Trothan Gilbertson, who Maggie befriends after he shows an interest in her profession of map-making. Cartography works well as a connection between the two of them, but also emerges as a way of showing that Maggie has become disconnected from her sense of identity and the fundamentals of her vocation. Whilst Trothan wanders the landscape, sketching with paper and pencil, Maggie toils on her computer trying to create an infographic that will show population growth in the Nigerian city of Lagos, with the assistance of Google Earth. This is modern cartography – remote, separated from source – and Maggie is conflicted by its efficiency versus the detail and precision of the traditional process of ink on coated glass plates or layers of plastic film. Using these methods, Trothan draws not only what is physically there, but also what he gleans from local gossip, so that his map begins to shape an accurate portrayal not only of the terrain but also of the close-knit, corrupt community.

As the thread of Maggie's past is drawn out, the novel really picks up pace and the undertow of the title becomes a rip tide. If there is a gripe, it's that Trothan's home-life never truly comes into focus. Fuller exploration would have sharpened both the character and Maggie's attachment to him. That said, it is pleasing that the 'tragic events' of her past subtly explore themes of loss and motherhood, rather than being over-stated. Cracknell's prose is well-judged and often sparkles with soft-spoken insight. This is a writer in control of her material: able to provide a mapped overview of a character caught between two lives, but with impressive layering that evokes her current feeling of dislocation within that – curiously Scottish – phenomenon of a small community in a sparse, vast landscape that is able to produce a suffocating insularity. Cracknell's novel is fully aware of the myth and folklore of the far North of Scotland but also of the impact of the contemporary world on that tradition. *Call of the Undertow* leaves you with unsettling questions about both the community Maggie has moved to

and the character herself and, after reading, you continue on with the kind of thoughtful, thousand-yard stare that you might gain after a long walk, buffeted by wind and chided by the birds, along the stretch of sand at Dunnet Bay, Caithness.

— *Noboru Wataya*

Oestrogen-fuelled Poetry

The Seed-box Lantern: New and Selected Poems
Diana Hendry

Mariscat Press, RRP £10.00, 112pp

If all poets were placed on a male-female continuum, Ted Hughes would be at one extreme and Diana Hendry would be at the other. Hers is an intensely female voice, fuelled as strongly by oestrogen as others are by testosterone. Her capacity for empathy, for entering into the experience of the 'other' extends well beyond the usual suspects: mother, father, child, lover. She gives us the sea's marriage with the sky; the spider's feelings, her struggle to understand an apple tree. Small fish are described as "changing colour like wives / anxious to please a capricious spouse".

Hendry is a renowned writer of children's books and uses the deep and intense emotions of childhood to good effect. In 'Song for the Sea of Crete', she describes the movement of the sea: "it's hurl at land – / a child's leap at its father". The Arkadi Ferry "comes back like morning itself or the mother / whose faithful return you childishly doubted". The words love and heart appear often in this collection but without any trace of sentimentality. In 'Soliloquy to a Belly', a poem on pregnancy, a woman lies "behind this belly / thin and cold". This hard edge to her writing is also evident in this extract from 'The Stranger' on childbirth:

One day I'll love you more
than I can guess. Right now, resentful, tired,
Undone, I love and hate you all in one,
Reclaim myself and watch you from afar
And wonder – wonder who on earth you are.

The next stanza begins: "We quarrel when you're in the bath. I slap / your face". Definitely not sentimental. There is a liberal sprinkling of delightfully comic and playful poems. 'Artemis, Still Hunting' gives one woman's failed attempt to pick up a man in a café. The 'Sunbathing Song', which is to be rendered to the tune of 'All of You' by Cole Porter, is hilarious. The rhyming of "farce" with "sandy arse" and the description of "toasted tits" are slow burners which warm the cold, dark Scottish winter.

The selected poems from earlier publications, dating back to 1995, have more internal rhymes, more alliteration and more grit alongside the pearls. However, the poems from 'Twelve Lilts: Psalms and Responses', which give P. Hately Waddell's Scots versions of the Psalms, and the poet's personal responses are more gentle and wise in tone, more akin to the new poems. The

first of the twenty-six new poems, 'How to Play the Piano', has an excellent description of what psychologists call 'flow' and will strike a chord with readers who have never played a musical instrument.

Although there are no explicit references to feminism, it exists as a pervasive undercurrent. In the poem about Caroline Herschel, the first woman to discover a comet, the tension between her caring role and her work as an astronomer is presented with great subtlety and intelligence. There are also two new poems on the theme of Jewish ancestry. The second, entitled 'Kaddish', a mourning prayer or blessing in Judaism, is for a mother from a daughter and shows great generosity of spirit. It is an interesting contrast with Allen Ginsberg's poem of the same name about his mother. It seems no coincidence that the last word in this collection is 'love'.

— *Kanga the Kangaroo*

Changing Viewpoints

The Cry
Helen FitzGerald

Faber and Faber, RRP £7.99, 320pp

Two shadows loom large over this, Helen FitzGerald's fourth novel. Making a sly nod to the 1988 Meryl Streep vehicle, *A Cry in the Dark*, where the parents of a missing baby find themselves in the unwanted spotlight of both public and legal judgement, and the more recent Madeleine McCann case, FitzGerald asks the question that we were all thinking: did they do it? It's both a strength and a weakness of this novel that FitzGerald answers the question so early in the narrative. Of course, there are twists and turns along the way, familial ties, sexual jealousies, and the desire to do the right thing propel the action forward and keep us guessing just enough for us to wonder where it's all heading. Again, the answer to this is revealed early on, so we are left with the titbits, and mildly salacious details of a marriage that is "built on pain the pain of another". Joanne, the mother of baby Noah, is a Scottish teacher holidaying with husband, spin doctor and aspiring Labour politician, Alistair in his native Australia, when the child is 'kidnapped'. There follows a police investigation, convincingly handled in its details, as well as a press furore which, though initially sympathetic , is spurred on by anonymous Internet bloggers and tweeters, and soon begins to sour. The novel is more of a no-but-yes-but-who-really -dunnit-really? than a straightforward whodunnit, and it is here that problems begin to arise: the question of which parent, Joanne or Alistair, did what – to – whom ceases to be of much interest since it's an obvious red-herring and, unless the reader has a great deal invested in Joanne as a character, the narrative struggles to maintain itself. This is hard to achieve when so much is given away so early, and neither Joanne nor Alistair really manage to generate the required sympathy. This much, at least, rings true when you consider FitzGerald's real-life counterparts – which may be her point. The novel's changing viewpoints – from Joanne to Alistair's wronged ex-wife Alexandra – also demand switching sympathies and for this reader at least, the narrative only really picks up when Alexandra does the talking. From the opening chapters, Joanne sounds more like a chic-lit heroine making her subsequent trauma somewhat hard to take, whereas Alexandra makes for grittier reading, but it doesn't take much doing to change perceptions of her from mad alcoholic to struggling single mother. The writing itself is pedestrian, doing just enough and no more, refusing to indulge in any real kind of liveliness. The pages turn easily enough though, and FitzGerald is successful when she turns to social media, effectively capturing the clamour of voices decrying Joanne as a failed mother, a murderer, nuts or just plain wicked. Alexandra's daughter Chloe is interesting too, but we don't get enough of her – I had hoped that her narrative might make an appearance at some point – only when glimpsed through Alexandra's eyes. As a psychological thriller, the novel feels like a slight offering when it could have been more, and FitzGerald seems to have missed the boat on what might have been a really juicy take on the media's reflection of our own prurient fascination with the suffering of others and quickness to judge. No doubt FitzGerald's fans will enjoy this novel, but for an idea with much meat on the bone, there's a little too much gristle for this dingo to chew on.

— *White Fang*

Northern Universes

The Universe is a Silly Place
Graham Fulton
Controlled Explosion Press,
RRP £5.00, 32pp

A Northerly Land
George Gunn
Braevalla Press
RRP £7.95, 60pp

Tender is the North
Sheila Templeton
Red Squirrel Press
RRP £4.00, 40pp

The Universe is a Silly Place by Graham Fulton has photos in its middle: stuffed toys looking out of aeroplane windows, wearing Andy Murray masks, leaning on Jeremy Beadle's grave. Unexpected in a poetry pamphlet and yes, silly, but then so are the situations that prompt Fulton's poems. 'Daleks at the *Free From* Section of Tesco' is "To be spoken in two separate voices. / One to be deep and menacing. / *One to be shrill and hysterical.*" and you find yourself reading the italicised lines in your best dalek voice. Fulton is matter of fact rather than mocking, observing and reporting back his take on the oddness of the everyday. Some poems are less bizarre and are read with a nod of recognition, sometimes a shrug. 'Masterchef', for example, describes standing on a piece of uncooked macaroni in the middle of the night and 'Spam' lists, exhaustively, titles of junk mail Fulton received over a few months but Fulton's attention to detail and energy come across in poems like 'Four Avocadoes of

the Apocalypse' and 'Welcome to Pointless' in which, while watching a game show, he realises "I'm redoing part of existence that / I've already done. / and the audience are laughing / in the same places,".

George Gunn's *A Northerly Land* is, at 60 pages, more full-length collection than pamphlet but the format is compact, fitting for poems that resemble miniatures of expansive landscapes. Gunn's passion for the far reaches of Scotland is palpable yet the poems are meditative in their detail: "Six weeks of gales have blown the tide / flat into the bay / a thin white line like shifting ice". This is 'The Winter Coast', a long poem that travels: "the marram grass rises up like eyelids / they blink a parabola of three miles / & by the faint light of these flickering runes / I see that nothing is shaped / but the sand by the wind / that we are ruled by barbarians". Punctuation is minimal throughout the collection and capital letters are confined to beginning a poem and place names, plotted here in 'Lighthouses': "we cross from Caithness to Orkney / as the Pentland Firth rises up / & consumes itself / to the West Swona & Stroma". There is intimacy too in 'September': "ageless black paths / signalled in the curls of your hair" and 'Kite': "the bindertwine which was too hold / to the Earth & to our father's hand" and in 'Two Otters' we are reminded: "our tomorrow will be different / but not impossible & we know / that the light will return".

Reading 'Auld Lang Syne' from Sheila Templeton's *Tender is the North* on New Year's Day gave me goose bumps as she describes the "heat of the kitchen" after sledging: "cocoa gritty with sugar / a stiff paste in the bottom of the cup" and milk for the morning porridge "...set out / in little bowls and cracked cups at night / so the cream rose and lay thick and cold." The poem ends, answering the Anne Michaels epigraph: "We are everything our mouths remember." Despite the big skies and darkness of the north ('Drifting', 'Lighten Up'), the poems in this collection contain warmth in abundance in their memories and experience of life and death. Humour too in 'Taking a Poet to Bed': "I am aware it's not good to be in bed alone, / in winter. So I asked Robert Burns /...,/ He suggested Derek Walcott. Who wasn't immediately / delighted". Scots vocabulary is lovingly peppered through the collection and while the last poems remember Zagreb, travel to Greece, honour a father dancing his daughter to sleep in Gaza, we return to a final poem written in Scots, 'Northsick': "... Hamesick...for frost riven the breath / fae ma breast, for that high sky, its white burnin mune, / the aipple green veils o the Merry Dancers.".

— *Fiver*

Avoiding Resolution

Paradises
Iosi Havilio

And Other Stories, RRP £10.00, 204pp

The follow-up to his 2006 debut *Open Door*, Iosi Havilio's *Paradises* takes his unnamed female narrator from the first book's surrealist, rural setting to the rotting slums of Buenos Aires. After her ageing lover Jaime is killed in a road accident, the narrator's house is repossessed and she is forced to move to the city with her young son Simon. She soon finds temporary work in the reptile house at the zoo, and a place to squat in a condemned apartment block which is owned by a dying old woman called Tosca, who starts paying the narrator to administer her daily morphine injections. From this semi-secure base the narrator moves through a city punished by floods, heatwaves, and outbreaks of meaningless violence. Even this precarious stability is soon threatened though, by the reappearance of her old friend Eloisa. Hedonistic and self-destructive, Eloisa draws her into a world of slum bars, decadent rich kids, drugs and alcohol, and a half-hearted plot to rob her current boyfriend Axel of his expensive collection of jewellery.

Havilio's episodic, detached form, with minor incidents described at length and seemingly significant moments skipped over in a line, recalls the standard patterns of the existentialist novel. He is content to let the idea of 'character development' fall to the side as the fictional device that it is, and even though it can be frustrating at times he avoids the easy resolution of events. For example, the narrator's son falls dangerously ill, poisoned by the berries from the paradise trees that give the book its title; but in the end he gets better. The narrator steals an iguana from the zoo and worries that she'll lose her job; but it's okay, because she doesn't get found out. She becomes sexually attracted to her friend Iris; but nothing happens, and

Iris goes back to her own country.

In general there is much to admire here. As the narrator says at one point, "I swallow my words and allow things to happen", and this detached pace allows Havilio to avoid any hierarchy of meaning or significance, so that the descriptions of mundane moments share the same focal intensity as more vivid or violent ones. However, these random bursts of bizarre imagery feel like an attempt to give the book a brooding, minatory (and Roberto Bolano-esque) tone that it never quite achieves, and the flat, affectless style is applied too inconsistently to be effective. There is a sense that the author cannot quite commit himself to this clinical tone, and the narrator lurches between the truly functional ("I quickly swallow three spoonfuls to meet the requirements of nourishment") to the needlessly lyrical (two teenagers seen "kissing like amoebas"). The gains the novel makes in its form and focus are offset by this incoherence.

Beth Fowler's translation certainly feels as if it has been faithfully rendered. It's a purely arbitrary criticism, but it does jar occasionally to read British-English slang like 'arse', 'sod', 'dosh' and so on in a South American novel. Objectively it would make no more sense to use 'ass' or 'dough' instead, but doing so would perhaps give the novel a more accurate flavour of its hemisphere than otherwise. In the end the narrator and Eloisa do make it to their much-discussed heist, but the equivocal conclusion to the novel threatens a third volume of the narrator's meandering adventures.

— *Montmorency*

New and Selected Puns

A Twist of Lime Street
Eddie Gibbons

Red Squirrel Press, RRP £6.99, 100pp

Eddie Gibbons likes a pun. These poems are shot through with them. (Punshots?) Titles include: 'Shopping Forecast', 'Wife of Pi', 'Love in the Time of Coreldraw', 'Death Shall Have No Dim Onion'... For me, it sometimes undermines the mood (or what I want the mood to be). In 'Dire Morphine', for example, about the poet's dying father, I didn't want a pun. A pun wouldn't help me.

Maybe puns help Gibbons. Maybe I'm the problem. His poetry is friendly, unpretentious and sincere. And who am I to say puns are cheap? I love puns in everyday speech. And there are good puns here. I liked it (sue me) in 'Modernist Love' when a gallery-goer asked his lover if she fancied "a quick Chagall." But in 'Your Poems' Gibbons tells us that he's "taking each line as it comes" and that's how it goes for the most part, for me, the poems skipping from verse to verse with plays-on-words, jokey rhymes and cultural references. He sacrifices the poem for the line. It doesn't hold together.

However, there are other times when the accumulation is more than the sum of its parts. 'Portrait of Ana Dali' has the suitably surreal, tumbling feeling of a dream, the images arriving like objects thrown, all at once, up into the air:

Her lemonade has developed amnesia.
Her maracas engage in a row.
Her Mercedes Benz is ablaze at both ends.
She is wearing a watch that says NOW!

This Wastelandish piling up of connotations works best in prose poems like 'The Gap' or 'Ringo Starry Rhymes'. Meanwhile, poems about Gibbons' twentieth century heroes, 'Tom Waits Meets Liberace' or 'Henri Rousseau Meets Frank O'Hara', create strange worlds of archetypes and icons, both more heightened and more pared back than in other poems. ("I'd like to do you in oils, Frank, / peeking through a bush on Seventh Avenue.") The memories of a Liverpool childhood tasted of Hovis to me, but 'Pantoum of the Opera', with words like "Nibelungen ring road", "Götterdämmerung" and "Norbert Dentressangle truck" evoked a grey, romantic Europe somewhere. 'Long Ago With Giacomo', with its rhymes of endless Italian names ("Agostini rode for Morini / when Tarquinio Provini / left to ride for Benelli") used language not for the tricks it can turn but for its simple, transporting power.

Gibbons is best at his most unadorned. He writes a lot about his father but the father poem that most moved me was the new 'Swarfega', because of its restraint. Washing his hands like his worker-father did, he finds that "for a moment my right hand is his / right hand washing my left." Here it is the physical world of grease and oil and overalls and of colours – blue, green, orange, black – that transports him.

I also liked the very short 'Why Buses Come in Threes', which takes a known idea with a meaning we think we understand but then surprises. In unassuming words (no puns) Gibbons explains the progress of the first bus (slow: lots of passengers) and the second (faster: fewer passengers) but then the third, the third is something else: it's darker, starker, weirder, and somehow funnier, and somehow profound.

— *Wol*

Old dog, new bones

Bones & Breath
Alexander Hutchison

Salt Publishing, RRP £12.99, 84pp

If poets were footballers, Hutchison would be someone like Antonio di Natale: an underrated master, well on in his career but still in his prime, with versatile deployment, technical mastery and a keen aim for goal.

Hutchison is rightly a poets' poet. The plaudits on the book jacket from Andrew Greig, August Kleinzhaler and AB Jackson make clear the high regard for his writing. But he sits below the public radar of contemporary poetry. This is unfortunate, because his work is so direct, so vital, so tender; his acute wit underpinned by sly fondness and joyous pokes at the mystery of existence.

Although many poems were familiar from live readings, magazines and the recent pamphlet *Tardigrade*, seeing them collected on paper reinforced my delight at the range of tone, language, form and subject matter that Hutchison launches into with his subtle gusto.

This 4ᵗʰ collection since 1978's *Deep-Tap Tree* (still in print in the USA, testament to his cult status), confirms Hutchison's output is about quality. With Andrew Greig, Tom Leonard and Larry Butler, he is a wild Scottish link to the American underground of the 1960s & 70s, and beyond to Creeley and Williams. Read him and be delighted.

— *Moby-Dick*

Life's Work

The Tailor of Inverness
Matthew Zajac

Sandstone, RRP £8.99, 288pp

A couple of Edinburgh Festivals ago I took a chance on a one-man show called 'The Tailor of Inverness' which turned out to be the best piece of theatre I saw at that year's Fringe. That one man was actor Matthew Zajac, and the show was incredibly personal, emotional and involving. But this is not the place to review theatre. Zajac has turned the story of 'The Tailor of Inverness' into a book, and I was fascinated to see if his story could move me on the page as it had on the stage.

The book is intensely personal, yet it is one which will speak to every reader to a greater or lesser degree. The titular tailor is Zajac's father, Mateusz, who came from

Poland to reside in Inverness where he cut his cloth accordingly, becoming well integrated as part of the local community, perhaps unsurprisingly focusing on the here and now rather than the past. The play, and now this book, are a result of Matthew's curiosity about his father's life before he settled in the Scottish Highlands, and what he uncovered touches on some of the most horrific and tragic times of the twentieth-century.

It's a terrible cliché to call a person's tale a 'journey', but in this case it is wholly apt. In fact what unfolds is a series of journeys and discoveries as Matthew has to find out not only things which his father wanted to forget, but which much of what was Eastern Europe wants to forget as well. Workcamps, anti-semitism, underage soldiers, Nazism, Stalinism, and all the horrors which were undertaken in the name of those ideologies, are touched upon as Matthew continues to pull on the string that was his father's secret life, increasingly unsure that he wants to follow where it is taking him.

What the book makes clear is that this is Matthew's story as much as it is his father's. The latter's life is put in context by the former's upbringing, which included biennial holidays to Poland to visit Uncle Adam. His father's voice is heard in various chapters, which have been transcribed from tape recordings, and here I feel that seeing the play has given me a distinct advantage as I can hear the voice in my head as I read. Where the book definitely triumphs over the play is that you can follow the travails back and forth across Europe, the Middle East and North Africa much easier than could ever be done in a theatre, where all the travel does become a bit of a blur.

The Tailor of Inverness is a tale about a specific family, in the most unusual way, but it is when talking about family that the story comes to life and real emotion is to be found and empathy felt. Our family secrets and lies may not be as extraordinary as Mateusz Zajac's prove to be, but they might, it's just that few of us have the inclination to find out, and this book may only convince us that it is better to let such sleeping dogs lie. I won't say here if Matthew Zajac feels this undertaking was worth it or not, but there is much emotional and familial turmoil along the way. What is clear is that his father's past became an obsession which gave this actor not only the role of his life, but an unexpected and incredible insight into the man who raised him. It is a life's work, which you have a feeling is not yet at an end.

— *Kes*

A conspiracy of nuns

In The Rosary Garden
Nicola White

Cargo, RRP £8.99, 320pp

In the Rosary Garden by Nicola White is the most recent winner of the Dundee International Book Prize. It's set in Ireland in the 1980s when the main character Ali, who is waiting for her exam results, finds a dead baby in the Rosary Garden of her old convent school. Ali is an extremely well drawn character; not always likeable but always sympathetic, and it is she who raises the book above that of another Irish novel about nuns, illegitimate pregnancies and dead babies. The author captures very subtly the uncertainty of that stage in someone's life: the boredom and drinking, the complexity of friendship, the frustration with parents and the regretted sex.

As a result of finding the baby, Ali is manipulated by a journalist, a former pupil of the same convent school, into becoming a spokesperson for her generation for better sex education. On a television talk show she clashes with a doctor who espouses the traditional view of chastity outside marriage and children within it, later punishing her by offering false testimony that the dead baby is hers. Detective Swan, who is investigating the baby's death, is also an interesting character with his own complex background although this is not as well resolved as it could have been, perhaps leaving the way open for another book. This novel is confidently written and nicely paced and you are very quickly drawn into Ali's life and the gothic nightmare that it becomes.

— *Aslan*

Victorian World

Unfashioned Creatures
Lesley McDowell

Saraband, RRP £8.99, 292pp

Lesley McDowell's second novel is a darkly Gothic tale of mental asylums, family secrets and illicit desires. Based on the life of Isabella Baxter Booth, a childhood friend of Mary Shelley, the novel juxtaposes her unraveling marriage, with all its attendant strains, with the faltering career of the fictional Dr Akexander Balfour, a fiercely ambitious psychiatrist with his own dark secrets. From the opening pages an atmosphere of dread pervades each scene. The writing, whilst wearing the research lightly, is rich in historical detail and full of suspense. Each meticulously observed detail seems darkly portentous, the dialogue hinting at buried resentments and fears.

Isabella's disintegrating relationship with her increasingly violent husband, and the terrifying fits from which he suffers, are portrayed with excruciating clarity; we can sympathise with her plight and understand the murderous impulses she sometimes feels towards him. Isabella can be an unreliable narrator, however, and when her perspective differs from Alexander's it can be difficult to know who to trust: a strength of the writing which creates added suspense. At the start of the novel Alexander seems the more logical, functional person, but we quickly become aware that his ambition, particularly when coupled with his lack of success or recognition, is skewing his perspective

and affecting his decisions to a dangerous degree. Both Isabella and Alexander struggle with addictions, to laudanum and alcohol respectively, and in the sections where they are under the influence – drunk or drugged – the writing is at its best. Heightened images and broken, chaotic phrasing emphasise the fragility of the characters' grasp on reality and, indeed, their own sanity. At times McDowell's elliptical style can be a little frustrating for the reader. Her characters can feel a little elusive, their motivations unknowable. The writing is strongly rooted in place, however, and the various settings of the story – Scotland, England, Belgium – are well written.

The twin narrative structure offers us alternating chapters from Isabella and Alexander; a chance to see them side-by-side as the story builds towards their first encounter. But coming almost halfway into the novel, the eventual meeting between them feels a little underwhelming, lacking in emotional impact, and the resulting dynamic between the two characters doesn't always convince. However as individuals Alexander and Isabella and their ruined lives are compelling, their voices convincing, and the writing, while describing heightened emotions and gripping events, never succumbs to melodrama. Unfashioned Creatures is a dark and fascinating window into a Victorian world of asylums, troubled relationships and addiction.

— *Richard Parker*

Dear Gutter

I'm in my early thirties and despite one major relationship lasting around three years, my love life is characterised by intense short-term affairs that I grow quickly bored of.

I'm a woman in my mid-thirties with a responsible professional job. I have a decent salary and a good quality of life. I have a wide circle of friends and enjoy my independence. But over the last few years I have failed to settle in to any kind of long-term relationship. Apart from one boyfriend who lasted three years, on and off, in my mid-twenties, all my affairs have been intense but short-lived. I love the energy of the first few months after meeting someone new but as things cool off I get bored and start to find fault. I'm a confident person and not afraid to have a one-night-stand when I'm in the mood. That's fine as far as it goes but I now feel ready to settle down into a more serious relationship. I don't know if I just haven't met the right person yet or if there's something wrong with me or my approach.

Gutter says

This is a common complaint from many people in their thirties who haven't met Mr or Mrs Right yet. At the heart of any long-term relationship is equality. I'm not just talking about your boyfriend doing his share of the housework and not behaving like a chauvinist pig. In any successful partnership it's vital that you are each other's equal intellectually, physically and emotionally. An imbalance of power, whether real or perceived, can create tension, insecurity and resentment. It can also result in negative, self-destructive behaviour in both partners.

You say that your relationships can be characterised as brief affairs that have, on the one hand, had an intensity that you crave but, on the other, have proved ultimately dissatisfying. I wonder if you are unconsciously sabotaging things for yourself from the outset. Sometimes we're physically attracted to people who don't challenge us intellectually or emotionally because this makes us feel secure and in control.

I must ask, are you assuming that just because you have a successful career and a good social life that, by rights, you should also have a fulfilling relationship? Salary and responsibility are no measure of emotional maturity. Perhaps at the heart of your brief encounters is a deep-seated insecurity about your own worthiness of love and that is keeping you from entering relationships with an open mind and an open heart. Instead you are grasping tight to control which is strangling things from the get-go. Once the novelty of a new sexual partner has faded you may be finding it impossible to take things forward because you are unwilling to meet them on an equal basis, with your defences down.

It may also be worth considering what kind of relationship you had as a child with your father. The way we relate to the objects of our affections can be greatly influenced by patterns established in our earliest years, particularly with parents of the opposite sex. It's a father's or mother's job to give us unconditional love, acceptance and affection while keeping us on the straight and narrow. But if your father was emotionally distant, inconsistent, manipulative or unpredictable it could make you, as an adult, crave the thrill of attention you were denied to the exclusion of all else. It might be worth asking yourself what attracts you most in your relationships. Is it love, respect and affection or the thrill of the chase?

Granted, you may have just been unlucky in meeting a series of men who, as you get to know them, have not come up to muster. But it may also be the case that you're looking in the wrong places for the wrong kinds of men. Without, I hope, sounding like something from the 1950s, an obstacle to intimacy can be the decision to start a physical relationship before you've got any kind of measure of a potential partner. As we all know, a sexual relationship develops its own unique momentum and it's easy to seek short term gratification with someone who, should you take the time to look a little closer, is clearly incompatible – because they don't share similar values, aren't open emotionally themselves or just aren't house-trained. There's nothing like discovering someone's annoying habits to dampen the ardour. We've all been in that situation, when the scales sudden fall from our eyes and we think, what the hell am I doing with this idiot? If you're the kind of person that enjoys being the hunter rather than the hunted then you may need to resist your carnal urges long enough to fully appraise just how suitable a potential lover might be.

Television, film and the broader media constantly bombards us with the message that we aren't a complete human being till we find our significant other. This of course places huge pressure on all of us to seek that imaginary perfect partner. However monogamy is so often dependent on timing, meeting someone who is travelling in roughly the same direction at the same time as we are that we're also lucky enough to find attractive and vice versa.

The way to give yourself the best possible chance of finding that special someone is to release yourself from the burden of expectation. Focus on making friendships instead. That way you might discover that Mr or Mrs Right is closer than you think.

If you have a problem you'd like advice on send it to *deargutter@gmail.com*

Contributor Biographies

Juana Adcock is a writer and translator working in English, Spanish and Spanglish. Her first poetry collection, *Manca*, was published early 2014 in Mexico. She is based in Glasgow.

Gregor Addison lives in Glasgow. His poetry was recently published in Carcanet's *Oxford Poets Anthology 2013*. He has also been published in various magazines, including *New Writing Scotland*, *Causeway*, *The Edinburgh Review*, *Chapman*, *Gairm*, *Gath*, and *Cabhsair/Causeway*. He is currently working on material for a new collection. He is the author of *Pure Wool*. Follow him on Facebook.

Helen Addy is from Forres in Morayshire. She was a Runner-Up in the 2013 BBC Proms Poetry Competition, and was Commended in the 2013 William Soutar Prize. Her work has appeared in various print and online journals such as *Ink, Sweat and Tears*, *Open Mouse*, *Anti-Zine*, *NEON*, *Ol' Chanty*, *Northwords Now*, *The Waterhouse Review*, and *From Glasgow to Saturn*.

Nick Athanasiou has been living in Glasgow since 2000. After retiring as an accountant at twenty-five, he returned to university to read literature. His play 'After Life' closed the Triliteral Festival in Nottingham in 2010. He hopes to complete his first (proper) novel this summer, or next. Or maybe the one after that.

William Bonar's pamphlet, *Frostburn Steel*, was published in 2004 by Dreadful Night Press and his poems have been published in a variety of newspapers, magazines and anthologies. A short sequence, 'Visiting Winter: A Johannesburg Quintet', published in Gutter 06, was chosen as one of the Best Scottish Poems of 2012.
scottishpoetrylibrary.org.uk/poetry/poems/visiting-winter-johannesburg-quintet

Margaret Callaghan is a writer and researcher who lives in Glasgow. She is currently working on a novel called *The Last Big Weekend of the Summer* which is about a group of friends in thier twenties whose relationship changes over one summer.

Jim Carruth is an award winning poet with six collections of poetry published to date. His most recent *Rider at the Crossing* was published by Happenstance Press in 2012. Last year he won Mclellan Poetry Prize. In 2005 he set up and currently chairs St Mungo's Mirrorball, a 180-strong network of Glasgow poets.

Frances Corr has been a new writer for about twenty years now. In an earlier life she wrote plays which made it to the stage and over the years has squeezed out some short stories and poetry which have made it to print. She is also an artist and is currently working on tiny oil paintings of interiors.

David Crystal was born in Prudhoe, Northumberland in 1963 and now lives and works in London and Edinburgh. He has had two previous collections from Two Rivers

Press. His latest collection *Wrong Horse Home* is available from tall-lighthouse.

David Forrest is a writer, software engineer and sometime particle physicist. He lives in Glasgow where he performs poetry and prose to small gatherings of polite people. He is presently writing a short story collection and a novel.

Martin Cathcart Froden stacks aubergines for a living. Originally from Sweden, he has lived in Canada, Israel, Argentina and London. His writing has been shortlisted for the Bridport Prize and broadcast on Radio 4. At the moment he's working towards an MLitt in Glasgow, where he lives with his wife and two small blonde people. www.lumawords.co.uk

Graham Fulton's poetry collections include *Humouring the Iron Bar Man* (Polygon), *Open Plan* (Smokestack Books), *Full Scottish Breakfast* (Red Squirrel Press), *Upside Down Heart* (Controlled Explosion Press) and *Reclaimed Land* (The Grimsay Press). New major collection *One Day in the Life of Jimmy Denisovich* is to be published by Smokestack Books this summer. Website: www.grahamfulton-poetry.com

J Johannesson Gaitán grew up in Sweden with interims across the pond in Colombia. She moved to Edinburgh to pursue her MSc in Literature and, quite fittingly, Transatlanticism. With her partner she maintains therookeryinthebookery.org, reviewing books in translation. Her stories and poems have appeared, or are forthcoming

in, *Far Off Places*, *Witness Magazine*, and *The Stinging Fly* among others.

New to poetry writing, **Lesley Glaister** has written thirteen novels, the most recent, *Little Egypt*, to be published by Salt in 2014. Her stories have been anthologised and broadcast on Radio 4. She has written drama for radio and stage. Lesley is a Fellow of the RSL, teaches creative writing at the University of St Andrews and lives in Edinburgh.

Charlie Gracie is from Baillieston, Glasgow and now lives near Stirling. His poetry and short stories have featured in a range of Scottish publications. He has collaborated with other artists, including a sculptor and an electronic improvisation band. His work is about dark places and the glimmer that lives there and about green places and what lies beyond the surface.

A Geordie, **Steve Harvey** has been an English teacher, police officer, volunteer teacher in Iraq and lecturer in Modern Poetry at Suleimaniyah University, Safety & Security Officer for an NGO in South Sudan, run the 'Children, Fathers & Fatherhood' Project in Scotland and creative writing courses in Normandy. He now organises events in Edinburgh, including poetry evenings in the Sheep Heid pub.

Kevin Henderson has been exhibiting and making performance art works internationally since the late 1980s; a selection of recent paintings were seen in the exhibition 'Drawn Away Together'

(Talbot Rice Gallery, Edinburgh, 2013) about current forms of abstraction in Scotland, while his poetry has been published in *Anon*, *Northwords Now* and *Gutter* as well as in a number of journals, catalogues and anthologies.
www.storkandhedgehog.wordpress.com

Linda Henderson lives in Skye. In the late nineties she started writing as a way of learning her new cultural landscape. A 2002 graduate of the Strathclyde/Glasgow Creative Writing Masters degree Linda has published in many journals and most recently, *Words from an Island* (Skye Reading Room). In 2006 she won the inaugural Books from Scotland Short Story Competition.

James Irvine is from Edinburgh and now lives in East Lothian. His first novel, *Changing Light*, is published on 30 April 2014.

Vicki Jarrett is a novelist and short story writer from Edinburgh. Her novel, *Nothing is Heavy*, was shortlisted for the Saltire Society First Book of the Year 2013. Her short fiction has been widely published and shortlisted for the Manchester Fiction Prize and Bridport Prize. She has recently finished a short story collection and is working on another novel.
www.vickijarrett.com

Brian Johnstone's sixth collection *Dry Stone Work* will be published by Arc in May 2014, his most recent having appeared in 2009. His poems have been translated into over 10 different languages and has appeared throughout the UK, in America and Europe. He is a founder of StAnza: Scotland's International Poetry Festival and was Festival Director from 2000-2010. Website: brianjohnstonepoet.co.uk

Shaunagh Jones is a short story writer and a graduate of the University of Glasgow's Creative Writing MLitt programme. Her work has been published online and in print.

Formerly a political lobbyist for the Convention of Scottish Local Authorities, **Lindsay Macgregor** has recently completed an MLitt in Writing Practice and Study at the University of Dundee. She co-hosts Platform, a regular poetry and music evening at Offtherails Arthouse, Ladybank.

Vicky MacKenzie lives in the East Neuk of Fife and teaches creative writing for the Open College of the Arts. Her poetry and short stories have won several awards including the Ruth Rendell Short Story Competition and the McLellan Poetry Prize. She has a PhD in poetry and science and is working on a novel about John Ruskin.

Kevin MacNeil is an award-winning author from Stornoway, now resident in London. Poet, novelist, playwright, cyclist, practising Zen Buddhist. Currently an Honorary Writer in Residence at Kingston University and Director of Poetry on the Struileag project. For more, visit KevinMacNeil.com or say hello on Twitter @Kevin_MacNeil

Sean Martin is a writer, poet and filmmaker. He holds an MA in Creative Writing from Edinburgh Napier University, and his books include studies of alchemy, gnosticism, the Knights Templar and Andrei Tarkovsky. He won the 2011 Wigtown Poetry Prize.

Katy McAulay's fiction has appeared in anthologies by New Writing Scotland, Luath Press, Leaf Books and Cargo, and on BBC Radio Four. She lives in Glasgow.

Marion McCready lives in Argyll, her poetry pamphlet collection, *Vintage Sea*, was published by Calder Wood Press (2011). She won a Scottish Book Trust New Writers Award in 2013 and won the Melita Hume Poetry Prize (2013). Her first full-length collection, *Tree Language*, will be published in the Spring 2014 by Eyewear Publishing.

John McGlade is a freelance writer from Glasgow. He scripts satirical and comedy material for television, radio and theatre shows across the UK. He writes stand-up for leading comedians, and also poetry which he performs around Scotland.

Carol McKay's fiction appeared in Gutter 1 and 9. 'War Bird' is her first poem in the magazine, though Freight published 'Transience' in their groundbreaking *Knuckle End* anthology. She also has poems in *Istanbul Review 4* and *From Glasgow to Saturn 32*. Carol teaches creative writing through The Open University, and won the Robert Louis Stevenson Fellowship in 2010. www.carolmckay.co.uk

In 2013, **Donal McLaughlin** was shortlisted for the Best Translated Book Award (USA). *Naw Much of a Talker* (Freight),

his Glaswegian version of a novel by Pedro Lenz, also appeared to rave reviews. His translations of novels by Arno Camenisch and Monica Cantieni are due this spring. As is *beheading the virgin mary & other stories* – his own new collection (Dalkey Archive). www.donalmclaughlin.wordpress.com

Hugh McMillan is an award winning poet from Penpont. His collected poems *Thin Slice of Moon* came out in 2013. He is currently working on a book commissioned by the Wigtown Book Festival on themes and stories in contemporary Dumfries and Galloway.

John Douglas Millar is a writer. He was born in Scotland. He lives in London.

Wendy Miller is a Glasgow-based writer, artist and teacher. She writes poetry and plays as well as teaching creative writing in HMP Barlinnie. Wendy wrote and directed *Even In Another Time* and co-wrote and directed *The Bridge*, both performed as part of Glasgay! She is currently working on her latest play, *Baby Steps*.

Stephen Nelson is the author of *Lunar Poems for New Religions* and *Flylyght* (Knives, Forks and Spoons Press), *Eye Jar* (Red Ceilings Press), and *YesYesY* (Little Red Leaves Textile Series). He contributed to *The Last Vispo Anthology* (Fantagraphics), and appeared recently in The Sunday Times Poet's Corner. Check his lovely blog of vispo and other writing at www.afterlights.blogspot.co.uk.

Wayne Price was born in south Wales but has lived in Scotland since 1987. His short stories and poems have won many awards in the UK, Ireland and America. His first short story collection, *Furnace*, was published by Freight Books in 2012.

Orcadian poet, **Olive M Ritch** has been published in a number of literary journals and anthologies including *The Hippocrates Prize 2011* and *Don't Bring Me No Rocking Chair*. She received a commendation in the National Poetry Competition 2003 and won the Calder Prize for Poetry at the University of Aberdeen in 2006.

Currently a Clydebuilt mentee, **Kay Ritchie** grew up in Glasgow and Edinburgh, lived in London, Spain and Portugal and worked as a photographer, teacher of English and radio producer. Settled back in Glasgow she has been published in *Tracks in the Sand, Shorelines, The Glad Rag, New Writing Scotland 31* and *Treasures*. She has performed at various event.

Samuel Derrick Rosen was born and raised in Glasgow. He believes that any form of completeness is ultimately deceptive.

Tracey S Rosenberg is a novelist and poet. She won the 2013 Mountaineering Council of Scotland poetry competition, and her work has been commended in the Yeovil Prize and the Frogmore Prize. Her debut pamphlet *Lipstick is Always a Plus* is published by Stewed Rhubarb Press. A literary festival junkie, she's Bookstalls Manager at the StAnza Poetry Festival.

Mark Russell's debut poetry pamphlet *Pursued by Well-being* is published by tall-lighthouse. He has poetry published in *Antiphon, The Frogmore Papers*, the windows of pubs in Dumfries, *Poetry Salzburg Review, Cake, Bliss* (Templar), and was shortlisted for the Bridport Prize in 2012. He has a thin online presence at: markrussellat.wordpress.com

Ethyl Smith is an avid reader, designer, holistic therapist, illustrator, teacher... But mainly ever hopeful wrestler with words. She writes and sometimes illustrates children's fantasy, short stories often in dialect, and historical novels set in 17th century Scotland.

Kathrine Sowerby is a poet with a background in fine art. A graduate of Glasgow School of Art's MFA programme and Glasgow University's MLitt in Creative Writing, she has been widely published and awarded prizes including a New Writers Award from the Scottish Book Trust.

Alan Spence is an award-winning poet and playwright, novelist and short story writer. He is Professor in Creative Writing at the University of Aberdeen. His most recent book is the novel *Night Boat*, published by Canongate. He and his wife run the Sri Chinmoy Meditation Centre in Edinburgh.

Richard W Strachan lives in Edinburgh. He has had fiction and reviews published in *New Writing Scotland, The Scottish Review of Books, The View From Here* and *Litro*, and in 2012 he was given a New Writers Award by the Scottish Book Trust.

Zoë Strachan is a novelist, short story writer and librettist. Her most recent novel, *Ever Fallen in Love*, was shortlisted for the Scottish Mortgage Investment Trust Book Awards and the Green Carnation Prize. She teaches on the Creative Writing programme at the University of Glasgow. 'Thicker Than Water' is an extract from her work in progress.

Simon Sylvester is a writer, teacher and occasional filmmaker. He has written more than 1,000 very short stories on Twitter, and his first novel, *The Visitors*, will be published by Quercus Books in 2014. He lives in Cumbria with the painter Monica Metsers and their daughter Isadora.

Judith Taylor comes from Coupar Angus, and now lives and works in Aberdeen. She is the author of two pamphlet collections, *Earthlight* (Koo Press, 2006) and *Local Colour* (Calder Wood Press, 2010) and her 'Poem on Gless' was a runner-up in the James McCash Scots Poetry Competition 2013.

Ruth Thomas's latest novel *The Home Corner* was published by Faber last year. Her debut novel *Things to Make and Mend* and short story collection *Super Girl* are also published by Faber. Her work has won and been short-listed for various awards including the Saltire First Book Award, John Llewellyn Rhys Award and Frank O'Connor International Short Story Award. She lectures in Creative Writing at St Andrews University.

Kate Tough received a Creative Scotland Professional Development Award in 2013 to develop her experimental poetry. She co-runs Shawlands' regular event, Poetry@The Ivory (all welcome). Her novel, *Head for the Edge, Keep Walking*, is out in summer 2014 with Cargo Publishing. It was awarded a Scottish Arts Council Writer's Bursary in 2009. katetough.com

Kate Tregaskis lives and works in Edinburgh. In the dim and distant past she studied Creative Writing at Glasgow, Strathclyde and then Edinburgh Universities. She has had short stories published in various magazines and anthologies. She is currently in the throes of completing her second novel.

Tim Turnbull, originally from Yorkshire, now resides in Perthshire. His poetry collections, including *Caligula on Ice*, are published by Donut Press. He has also produced stage shows and is currently working on a PhD at Northumbria University among other projects.

Lynnda Wardle was born and grew up in Johannesburg. She has lived and worked in Glasgow since 1999. In 2007 she received a Scottish Arts Council award to write a novella about Africa. She has had poems and stories published in various magazines, most recently, *thi wurd*.

Zoë Wicomb is a South African writer who lives in Glasgow where she is Emeritus Professor in English Studies at Strathclyde University. Her work is widely translated in Europe and into Japanese. In 2013 she was awarded Yale University's inaugural Windham-Campbell Prize for fiction. Her novel, *October*, will be published in March 2014 by The New Press, New York.

Edinburgh-born poet, publisher and Chair of StAnza, **Colin Will** lives in Dunbar. His sixth collection, *The propriety of weeding*, was published by Red Squirrel in 2012. A Hawthornden Fellow, his full-length collection of haibun, *The Book of Ways*, will be published in 2014. His publishing house, Calder Wood Press, specialises in poetry chapbooks.

Jim C Wilson's writing has been published widely for over 30 years. His four poetry collections are *The Loutra Hotel*, *Cellos in Hell*, *Paper Run* and *Will I Ever Get to Minsk?* He was a Fellow of the Royal Literary Fund from 2001 to 2007 and has taught his Poetry in Practice course at Edinburgh University since 1994. More information at www.jimcwilson.com